HOUGOUMONT

The Key to Victory
at Waterloo

BY
JULIAN PAGET
AND
DEREK SAUNDERS

LEO COOPER
LONDON

Also by Julian Paget

COUNTER-INSURGENCY CAMPAIGNING
LAST POST: ADEN, 1964–67
THE STORY OF THE GUARDS
THE PAGEANTRY OF BRITAIN
THE YEOMAN OF THE GUARD
DISCOVERING LONDON CEREMONIAL AND TRADITIONS
WELLINGTON'S PENINSULAR WAR

First published in Great Britain in 1992 by
LEO COOPER,
190 Shaftesbury Avenue, London WC2H 8JL
an imprint of
Pen & Sword Books Ltd.
47 Church Street, Barnsley, S. Yorks S70 2AS

A CIP catalogue record for this book is available
from the British Library

ISBN: 0 85052 341 9

Printed in Great Britain by Butler & Tanner Ltd., Frome, Somerset

Contents

Maps and Illustrations

Foreword
by General Sir David Fraser, GCB OBE DL

In all the many accounts of the Battle of Waterloo, Hougoumont takes a special place in the narrative. Hougoumont – château, garden, farm buildings, yard, orchard and wood – was the anchor that held firm the right of Wellington's Allied line. While he possessed Hougoumont – a strongpoint, as he made it, somewhat in front of the right of the main position and on lower ground – Wellington knew that Napoleon would have to make a long and vulnerable march if he wished to outflank the Allied right; he had no chance, until he had occupied Hougoumont, of smashing that right by frontal assault; and he would be constricted, by Allied possession of La Haye Sainte and Hougoumont, in the frontage of attack he could develop against the Allied centre. Hougoumont was one of the principal keys to the position, and the Regiments whose men died in considerable numbers to defend the place will always remember its name.

For the fighting at Hougoumont was arduous and bloody; and – in this, unlike other sectors of the front on that memorable Sunday, 18 June – it went on almost without respite from the first attacks by Jerome Bonaparte's Division to the closing stages of the battle; light beginning to fade, casualties on both sides enormous, exhaustion near overcoming the long-suffering troops, Napoleon's final, frustrated offensive defeated, and the Guard retreating in disarray past Hougoumont's woods and walls.

Until that moment the defenders of Hougoumont seldom had many minutes of calm. They were reinforced again and again by companies from the main position, their enemies broke once

1

into the heart of the defended area and threatened to do so again and again, French artillery pounded them savagely, French attacks besieged them on three sides, supplies were difficult and dangerous to come by. But through the long hours of Waterloo, Hougoumont held.

'No troops but the British,' Wellington said afterwards, 'could have held Hougoumont, and only the best of them at that.' It is thoroughly fitting that justice is now done to that heroic 'battle within a battle' by Julian Paget, himself a Coldstreamer, and Derek Saunders. For the brunt of the defence of Hougoumont was borne by the Foot Guards – the Light Companies of all three Regiments, and then, through the height of the fighting until its close, by the companies of the Coldstream and Third Guards fed into the battle in succession until virtually the whole of the two battalions of the 2nd Guards Brigade were deployed there.

'No troops but the British, and only the best of them at that.' No dispassionate reader of this epic story will feel inclined to challenge the great Duke's verdict.

Preface

The Duke of Wellington himself declared that 'the outcome of the Battle of Waterloo rested upon the closing of the gates at Hougoumont', and there is no doubt that the defence of Hougoumont was crucial to the final victory. Yet this dramatic story has never been fully told, despite the hundreds of volumes that have been written about Waterloo. This book, which includes material from a number of unpublished archives, is an attempt to fill the gap.

The buildings at Hougoumont today are not exactly as they were in 1815; the Château and several outbuildings have disappeared, and the shape of the North Gate has changed. The well-head and some walls have gone, and an extension has been built on the south side of the Gardener's House. But the overall layout remains little changed, so that it is easy to envisage the bitter fighting that took place there.

The landscape too has altered. The small wood to the south of Hougoumont has been removed, as have all the orchards; a new wood has been planted on the ridge to the north, while the area there that was held by Byng's Brigade is now an access road to the motorway. Several other roads and tracks have also changed from those existing in 1815. The formal garden of Hougoumont is now a meadow, and the avenue of trees from the North Gate to the Nivelles road has disappeared.

But there are, thankfully, few new buildings in the immediate area, and it is still possible to envisage the scene as it was on 18 June, 1815. It is a very moving experience to walk round Hougoumont, particularly when one knows something of the events of that day.

It has not been easy to compile a clear account of just what happened at Hougoumont; it is not even certain exactly what troops were involved, and in the confusion of the non-stop struggle, no one could be sure of timings, what orders were issued, when, and by whom. Personal accounts of events by those who were there differ as widely as the analyses of historians since.

This account is based on detailed research of many sources, but it is not claimed to be by any means the final, indisputable answer; it is our assessment of what we think happened. Derek Saunders, who has collaborated with me in this research, is one of the most knowledgeable authorities on Waterloo, and on Hougoumont in particular. He has not only spent a lifetime investigating every detail, but has also devoted many summer holidays to checking events on the ground, and also carrying out digs at Hougoumont – in the course of which he re-discovered and excavated the draw-well. He has now opened a Waterloo Museum at Crow Hill in Broadstairs, Kent, and anyone interested in the battle should certainly pay it a visit.

Many others have helped us compile this story of Hougoumont. We have had much support from Madame Anne Appels of the Wellington Museum at Waterloo, which is a vital part of any visit to the battlefield, ideally *before* one walks round. Lucien Gerke, the curator there, has also provided invaluable material on the history of Hougoumont and on the French side of the story, as has Philippe de Callatay. Comte Dominic de Grunne, whose ancestor was largely responsible for ensuring that the battlefield was preserved as a national monument, has been most helpful, as has Baron Jean Bloch of the Waterloo Committee in Belgium.

We would like to express our humble thanks to Her Majesty The Queen for gracious permission to reproduce from the Royal Collection the illustration on page 71.

We are also most grateful to the following for permission to reproduce illustrations in their possession: Christopher D'Ambrumenil; The National Museums of Scotland; The Cavalry and Guards Club; The National Army Museum; the Trustees of the Wellington Museum, Apsley House; and the Wellington Museum at Waterloo.

Finally, we are most grateful to Diana Paget and Mary Varney for taking all the photographs of Hougoumont as it is today.

Chapter 1
Château de Hougoumont

The modest château and farm of Hougoumont lie in a hollow just below the ridge of Mont St Jean, some 12 miles south of Brussels. The property dates back to the fourteenth century, and would probably have remained unknown to history had not the Battle of Waterloo taken place around it on 18 June, 1815. In the event, it was the scene of nine hours of bitter fighting, and some 6,500 men were killed or wounded attacking or defending it.

The original name was 'Goumont',[1] which is said by some to derive from the resin or 'gomme' that was produced by the large pine trees growing on the high ground round the château. This gave rise to the name 'Gomme Mont' (or 'Resin Hill'), which later became 'Gomont' or 'Goumont', and by 1815 'Hougoumont'. A 'Bois de Goumont' is mentioned on several 17th century maps of the area, as is a château and a farm.

The property was acquired in 1661 by a family called Arazola de Onate, who later added 'Gomont' to their title. They occupied the château for 130 years, but in 1815 the owner was a Chevalier de Louville; he, however, was then 86 and lived in Nivelles; Hougoumont was let to a tenant farmer, whose name was Antoine Dumonceau. The chateau was at this time unoccupied and unfurnished.

Hougoumont consisted in 1815 of a compact group of buildings round two courtyards and largely enclosed by walls.

The **Château** was in the centre, and was noticeably higher

---

[1] 'Gomont', 'Gomant' and 'Gomon' also appear.

Château de Hougoumont before 1815.

than the other buildings. It was not particularly large, being only two storeys high, and an unusual feature was a tall, narrow tower to one side, which contained a staircase and had an attractive, four-sided roof, topped by a weather-vane. A watercolour in the Guards Museum in London shows the château as being cream-coloured.

To the east of the château was the **Farmer's House**, a handsome two-storeyed building extending up to the garden wall.

Next to the château on the south side was a small **Chapel**; it was only 14 foot by 18 and was evidently intended solely for the use of the family. It was of red brick, built in much the same style as the château and the tower, and inside above the door was a 15th-century wooden figure of Christ crucified.

Along the west side of the property ran the **Great Barn**, which contained within it a carriageway that made a link between the two courtyards. The only other access between them was a

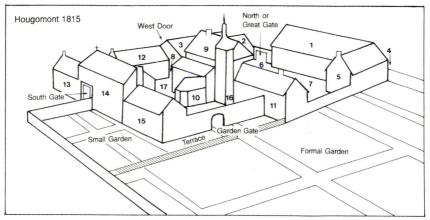

Layout of Hougoumont in 1815.

1	Cow house	9	Château
2	Open shed	10	Chapel
3	Great barn	11	Farmer's house
4	Shed	12	Stables
5	Cow house	13	Shed
6	Draw well	14	Gardener's house
7	Farmyard	15	Stable and office
8	Archway	16	Tower stairway

narrow archway and gate in the wall between the Great Barn and the west side of the château.

In the Northern Courtyard was a **Draw Well** with a distinctive well-head, some 10 foot high, and surmounted by a dove cot.

The south or enemy side of Hougoumont consisted of the **Gardener's House**, with stables and stores on either side. Under the house was an archway wide enough to take farm carts and secured by a pair of heavy, wooden gates. The archway led to an open area, some 30 yards square, beyond which lay a small wood.

In front of the Gardener's House was a **Small Garden** within the South Wall.

Entrances to Hougoumont

The four entrances to Hougoumont were clearly of great importance to its defence; otherwise the property was completely enclosed by walls.

The **South Gate**, running through the Gardener's House, was strongly built and also barricaded. There was much heavy fighting round it, as it faced the enemy, but it was never forced, and the buildings were never penetrated by the French.

Nearby, to the east, was a small **Garden Gate**, giving access to the **Formal Garden**; being inside the defences, it was never threatened, although under fire at times, and it was used to move troops back and forth into the garden.

On the west side of the Great Barn was a small door, usually called the **West Door**; it was important because it led into the lane along the west side of the farm, but it was never forced by the enemy.

The main entrance to Hougoumont was the **North Gate**, sometimes called the **Great Gate**, which led out to the Nivelles road. It consisted of two large wooden panels which swung together and were then held in position by a heavy wooden bar. It was for this reason that Wellington spoke of the closing of the gates (rather than the gate), and we will follow his example in this narrative.

Just to the west of the North Gate was a large open-fronted cart shed that extended from the Great Barn up to the North Wall; it was slightly lower than the Great Barn, but overlooked the North Gate, and so played a part in its defence.

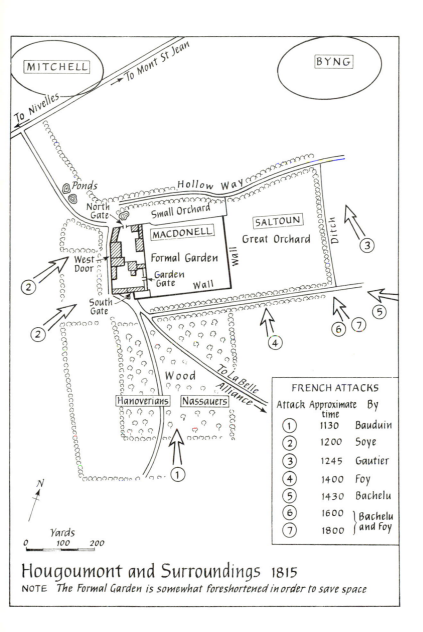

MITCHELL

To Mont St Jean

BYNG

To Nivelles

Ponds

Hollow Way

North Gate

Small Orchard

SALTOUN

MACDONELL

Great Orchard

Ditch

West Door

Formal Garden

Wall

③

②

Garden Gate

Wall

②

South Gate

④

⑤

⑥ ⑦

To La Belle Alliance

Wood

Hanoverians

Nassauers

N

①

FRENCH ATTACKS		
Attack	Approximate time	By
①	1130	Bauduin
②	1200	Soye
③	1245	Gautier
④	1400	Foy
⑤	1430	Bachelu
⑥	1600	} Bachelu
⑦	1800	} and Foy

Yards

0   100   200

Hougoumont and Surroundings 1815

NOTE *The Formal Garden is somewhat foreshortened in order to save space*

The Surroundings to Hougoumont

The ground to the *South* was particularly significant in 1815, as this was the most likely direction for any French attack. Immediately to the south of Hougoumont was a **Wood**, some 350 yards deep by 280 yards wide, which ran down into the valley where Reille's corps were assembled. This valley, running east to west, was of considerable importance in the battle because it could have been used by Napoleon as a line of advance to outflank Wellington's position on the ridge of Mont St Jean. The Duke was well aware of this possibility, and it was one of the reasons why he placed such stress on the importance of holding Hougoumont.

Between the north edge of this wood and the walls of Hougoumont was a gap of some 30 yards of open ground, and this proved a formidable obstacle to the attacking French, for, as they emerged from the wood, they met such a devastating musket fire from the buildings that they could never close in on the defences.

Three tracks ran from the south-west corner of Hougoumont. One went due south through the wood, one ran south-east towards Le Belle Alliance, while the third went along parallel to the southern edge of the garden.

To the *West* of Hougoumont was a small ridge and the French placed several guns there, which caused some trouble to the defenders. The ground on that side was also open and well suited to cavalry, which increased the threat of an attack from that direction.

Along the *North* edge was a sunken track, known as the **Hollow Way** (or Covered Way), which was to play a major part in the defence of Hougoumont because it was the supply route between the farm and the main Allied positions.

Immediately to the *East* of the farm buildings was a large **Formal Garden**, enclosed on the east and south sides by a brick wall and on the north side by a thick hedge and a ditch. It was laid out in the fashion of the time with box hedges, gravel or turf paths, and along the west edge was a terrace looking out across the garden.

Beyond the garden was the **Great Orchard**, with the Hollow Way running along its north edge, and the south and east sides lined by thick hedges.

For four centuries or more life had continued placidly and uneventfully at the Château de Hougoumont, but this was all to change dramatically in June, 1815.

Chapter 2
'The Devil is Unchained'

The *New Year of 1815* saw Europe enjoying a long-awaited period of peace after a quarter of a century of fighting against Napoleon Bonaparte. There was general relief that he was safely out of the way at last, exiled to the Mediterranean island of Elba, and it was hoped that he would trouble the world no more. Then, on *1 March, 1815*, Napoleon escaped and landed in France at Golfe Juan near Cannes.

'The devil is unchained,' wrote the British Commissioner on Elba, Sir Neil Campbell, adding somewhat unhelpfully that he thought the Emperor would head for Italy. In fact Napoleon made straight for Paris, which he entered in triumph on *20 March*.

The Allies (England, Prussia, Russia and Austria) refused to recognize him again as Head of State, whereupon he set about raising a new Grande Armée of 500,000 men to achieve recognition by force of arms.

In response, the four Allies agreed to provide 150,000 troops each, with a view to crushing Napoleon once and for all. This force could not, however, be raised before July, and the only effective troops available in the meantime were a very mixed international army of 83,000 under the Duke of Wellington and 125,000 Prussians under the gallant, 73-year-old Marshal Blücher. By June they were deployed along the Belgian frontier with France, and Wellington set up his headquarters in Brussels.

15 June 1815

He expected to receive enough warning of any move by Napoleon to be able to deploy his troops in time to deal with the threat. So, while the regiments guarding the frontier were on full alert, the lucky ones in Brussels could relax. Indeed, on *15 June* many of the officers were looking forward to attending the splendid Ball that the Duchess of Richmond was giving that night in honour of the Duke. It was to be held in the empty workshops of Simon, the coachbuilder, which were situated in the Rue de la Blanchisserie behind the Richmonds' house in the Rue des Cindres.

But at dawn on 15 June Napoleon's striking force of 125,000 confident veterans crossed the Belgian frontier and within hours had occupied Charleroi. They achieved complete surprise, and it was 3 o'clock that afternoon before Wellington at his headquarters at 544, Rue Royale in Brussels even heard of the invasion. It was important to maintain public morale, and he therefore went, albeit somewhat uneasily, to the Ball.

Then at around midnight came news that Napoleon was advancing in the direction of Brussels. Wellington ordered his officers to leave quietly and rejoin their units, but inevitably the party broke up amid scenes of anguish and alarm.

Wellington slipped away with the Duke of Richmond to the latter's dressing room where they both studied a map.

'Napoleon has humbugged me, by God,' Wellington declared. 'He has gained 24 hours march on me.'

'What do you intend to do?' asked the Duke.

'I have ordered the army to concentrate at Quatre Bras,' came the reply, 'but we will not stop him there, and if so, I must fight him here.'

He then placed his thumb nail over a small village on the map called Waterloo, some nine miles south of Brussels.[1]

---

[1] The actual battlefield is some three miles south of Waterloo.

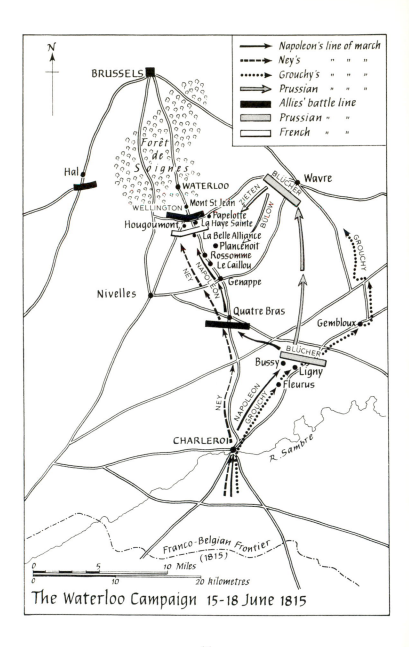

The Waterloo Campaign 15–18 June 1815

16 July 1815

Napoleon's plan was bold and simple. He intended to separate Wellington's and Blücher's armies by thrusting at a point between them. He would then attack the Prussians and drive them eastwards, away from the British. That done, he would turn on Wellington, defeat him and advance on Brussels.

To achieve this, he divided his army into two. He sent Marshal Ney with 20,000 men to seize the vital crossroads at Quatre Bras and so open up the road to Brussels. He himself led the main body of 78,000 against Blücher's 84,000 at Ligny.

Quatre Bras

At Quatre Bras it was touch and go all day. Ney launched a series of attacks, and the outnumbered Allies fought a desperate defensive battle. Units were rushed forward and then thrown into battle as soon as they arrived. Casualties were heavy, and the Gordon Highlanders, for example, lost twenty-five officers out of thirty-six. Wellington himself was nearly captured by French cavalry, and had to jump his horse into the Gordon Highlanders' square to escape.

Finally, late in the afternoon, two Guards Brigades arrived from Enghein, having marched for fifteen hours in the fierce heat. But they counter-attacked and, by dusk, the French had been driven back and Quatre Bras was still in Allied hands.

Ligny

Meanwhile at 2.30 in the afternoon Napoleon launched his attack against Blücher's 84,000 men six miles to the east. The Prussians fought gallantly, but were finally forced to withdraw northwards to Wavre with 12,000 casualties, compared to 8,500 French.

But the indomitable Marshal Blücher took the decision nevertheless that his next move would *not* be eastwards, as Napoleon expected, but westwards, so that he could join up with Wellington as he had promised. As is well known, the outcome of the Battle of Waterloo depended on this action, and Wellington later described it as 'the decisive moment of the century'.

17 June, 1815

Allied Retreat

The next day, Saturday, 17 June, was one of depressing retreat for the Allies. Wellington rode early that morning to Quatre Bras, still in ignorance of the Prussian defeat at Ligny. The news finally reached him about 10 am, and his typically laconic comment was, 'Old Blücher has had a damned good licking and gone back to Wavre, 10 miles. As he has gone back we must go too. I suppose in England they will say we have been licked. I can't help it; as they are gone, we must go too.'

So the Allied Army began marching back from Quatre Bras, some nine miles, to a position on the ridge of Mont St Jean, just south of Waterloo. As they trudged back, a heavy thunderstorm broke, adding to their misery and discomfort.

The French followed them, and, as darkness fell that evening, both armies took up position within sight of each other, astride the road to Brussels. The French extended either side of an inn called La Belle Alliance, while the Allies were across the valley, a mere 1500 yards away along the ridge of Mont St Jean.

At their respective headquarters the two greatest military commanders of the age planned their next move. Napoleon, at Le Caillou, was supremely confident that he would soon be in Brussels. Wellington, in the Bodenghein Inn at Waterloo, knew that his aim must be to hold out until Blücher arrived.

The fate of Europe depended on the outcome.

Chapter 3
'Keep Hougoumont'

The Battle of Waterloo was, surprisingly, the first time that Wellington and Napoleon confronted each other. Both were aged 46 and at the height of their powers; both were acknowledged masters of their profession. The outcome of the encounter would depend largely on the generalship of the two commanders before and during the battle, and also on the courage and resolution of the 140,000 troops involved. Whatever happened, it was bound to be (to quote one of Wellington's favourite phrases) 'a damned near run thing'.

Napoleon's Plan

Napoleon had 72,000 men, with 250 guns, and he also held the initiative. He had little doubt that he could without great difficulty overwhelm the scratch Allied army facing him, just as he had thrashed the Prussians at Ligny. He had sent Marshal Grouchy with 33,000 men to hold off Blücher to the East, and so discounted the possibility of the Prussians joining up with Wellington. He assumed that he now faced only the Allied army of 68,000 troops with 220 guns.

He particularly wanted to defeat Wellington, because the Duke was the only Allied commander whom he had not yet faced and beaten. He told his Chief of Staff, Marshal Soult, who had fought through most of the Peninsular War of 1807–14, 'Because you have been defeated by Wellington, you think him a great general. I tell you that he is a bad general, that his English are bad troops, and that this will be a picnic.'

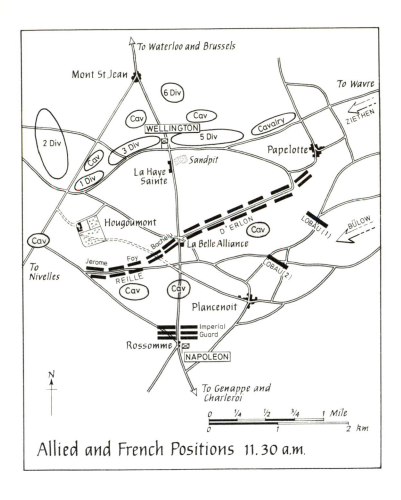

To Waterloo and Brussels

Mont St Jean

To Wavre

6 Div

ZIETHEN

Cav

Cav

Cavalry

WELLINGTON

2 Div

5 Div

Cav

3 Div

Papelotte

Sandpit

Cav

La Haye
Sainte

1 Div

Hougoumont

D'ERLON

Cav

LOBAU(1)

BÜLOW

Bachelu

La Belle Alliance

Cav

Jerome

Foy

LOBAU(2)

To
Nivelles

REILLE

Cav

Cav

Plancenoit

Imperial
Guard

Rossomme

NAPOLEON

N

To Genappe and
Charleroi

0   ¼   ½   ¾   1 Mile

0   1   2 km

Allied and French Positions 11.30 a.m.

He was confident that he could achieve victory by launching
a massive attack straight down the main road, having first de-
moralized the enemy with one of his famous artillery bombard-
ments. Marshal Soult ventured to suggest from much bitter
experience that it was unwise to attack British infantry head-on,
and he proposed instead an out-flanking movement round the

20

Château de Hougoumont, but his suggestion was scornfully rejected.

With a frontal assault in mind, Napoleon concentrated his 72,000 men on a front of about two miles on the ridge either side of La Belle Alliance. He put D'Erlon's Corps of 16,000 to the east of the main road and Reille's 15,000 to the west. Behind them were some 15,000 cavalry, ready to exploit the expected breakthrough. In reserve was Lobau's Corps, and under his own hand at Rossomme he kept his faithful, invincible Imperial Guard.

'We have ninety chances in our favour,' he declared, 'and not ten against.'

Wellington's Plan
Wellington could not be sure what the French would do, and he was also well aware that he himself had little option but to fight a defensive battle. He was outnumbered and out-gunned, and, above all, he was up against Napoleon. He knew that the only possible course was to hang on until Blücher and his Prussians[1] arrived; then, and only then, might he be able to take the initiative.

He was satisfied with the defensive position he had chosen a year earlier. It blocked the direct route to Brussels, and he had a good reverse slope where he could keep his men out of sight and also protect them from the worst of the inevitable French artillery bombardment. His main concern was to safeguard his right flank against the two possible moves that he expected Napoleon might make. The first was to use the dead ground round Hougoumont to make an out-flanking attack (as suggested by Soult) and so come in behind the Mont St Jean position from the west. The second was to advance north-west straight to the coast, and so cut off the entire Allied force from their ports and bases.

Wellington was also worried about the reliability in battle of his hastily assembled army. He had only some 24,000 British

[1] Bülow (40,000) and Ziethen (30,000).

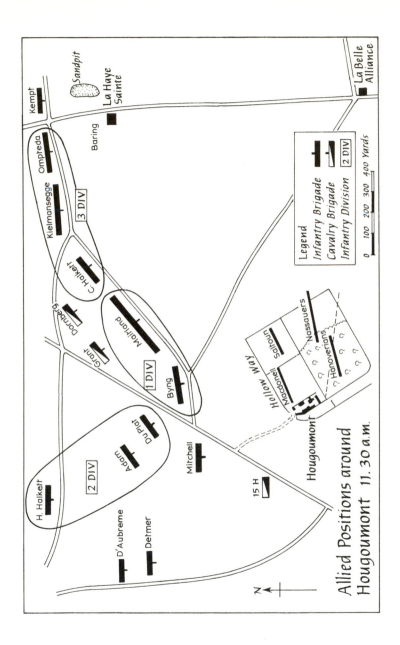

Allied Positions around Hougoumont 11. 30 a.m.

Legend
Infantry Brigade
Cavalry Brigade
Infantry Division 2 DIV

0 100 200 300 400 Yards

Regular troops, and less than half of them had seen active service. He could rely on the King's German Legion, but they were only 6,600 strong. The remaining 35,000 were a mixture of Belgian and Dutch troops, some of whom had been fighting *for* Napoleon in earlier years. He had little confidence in them, and so discreetly placed British brigades alongside them wherever possible in an attempt to avoid any weak points in the line. It was in his view an 'infamous army' compared to his magnificent Peninsular Army.

He positioned his 68,000 troops in a line some $2\frac{1}{2}$ miles long spread along the ridge running through Mont St Jean and centred on the road from Charleroi to Brussels. They were roughly opposite the French positions, and the forward troops of each side could see clearly what their enemy was doing 1,500 yards away across the valley.

Wellington divided his front into three sectors. The left, where he expected the Prussians to arrive, was thinly held with light cavalry and the 5th Division, which had suffered heavy casualties at Quatre Bras; this division was under the fiery General Picton, who was also in command of that sector. The centre was held by Alten's 3rd Division, and was commanded by the young Prince of Orange, but with Wellington keeping a close eye on him.

The third sector was his vulnerable right flank, and this he put under the ever-reliable Lord Hill. He made Cooke's 1st Division responsible for the defence of the Château de Hougoumont and the ridge immediately behind it, and also placed Clinton's 2nd Division in depth behind the 1st Division.

Finally, he detached Colville's 4th Division of 17,000 men with 30 guns to Hal (see map on page 16) in order to block any enemy thrust in that direction. This was a force that he could ill afford to spare during the forthcoming battle, but he regarded it as an essential precaution to protect his right in this way.

Looking at his main position, Wellington picked out three groups of buildings, all slightly forward of the ridge, which he considered it was vital to hold and to deny to the enemy. On the left was the farm of **Papelotte**, and he allotted the defence of that to the 2nd Brigade of Nassauers[2] (less one battalion who were sent to reinforce Hougoumont).

In the centre was the farm of **La Haye Sainte**, a key bastion covering the main road to Brussels, and he entrusted its defence to 360 men of the 2nd Light Battalion of the King's German Legion under Major Baring.[3] To support them he placed two companies (about 160 men) of the 95th (Rifles) in and around the adjacent sandpit, with a third company just behind them.

On his vulnerable right flank was the **Château de Hougoumont**, which he had made the responsibility of Cooke's 1st Division. Byng's 2nd Guards Brigade was on the ridge immediately north of Hougoumont, and the Duke also ordered the four light companies of 1st and 2nd Guards Brigades (some 400 men) to move forward and occupy the farm and the ground round it. In addition he brought Mitchell's Brigade[4] (from Colville's 4th Division at Hal), right forward and placed it northwest of Hougoumont astride the Nivelles road. Finally, he positioned a squadron of the 15th Hussars[5] on the same road, west of the farm.

These moves completed, he could only wait for the answer to two key questions. Would Napoleon try to outflank him to the west of Hougoumont or not? And would Blücher's Prussians arrive in time?

The Earl of Uxbridge, who had been nominated as Wellington's Second-in-Command, is said to have asked him what was the material point of his plan, so that he (Uxbridge) would know what to do should any accident befall the Duke. The reply he is said to have received was, 'Keep Hougoumont'.

---

[2] Commanded by Prince Bernard of Saxe-Weimar.
[3] From Colonel Ompteda's 2nd K.G.L. Brigade.
[4] It consisted of: 1/23rd Royal Welsh Fusiliers.
      3/14th Buckinghamshire Regiment.
      1/51st 2nd Yorkshire West Riding (Light Infantry).
[5] In support of Mitchell's Brigade.

Chapter 4
'A Miserable Night'

There was much unusual activity around Hougoumont through-out Saturday, 17 June. Staff officers galloped back and forth, particularly along the ridge of Mont St Jean, and several of them came and had a quick look at the château. Waggons loaded with stores and equipment trundled along the roads and tracks, while groups of soldiers, some mounted, some on foot, kept march-ing in from the south, where there was the sound of gunfire.

Rumours were flying around that Bonaparte was advancing on Brussels with a huge army and that he had already beaten the Prussians. This alarming news seemed to be confirmed by the stream of wounded soldiers, British, German, Dutch and Belgian, who were straggling back down the road from Quatre Bras. It was extremely sultry, with thunder in the air, and there was a general sense of foreboding, with trouble of some sort impending.

The farmer and his family had fled, and the only people remaining in the Château and farm at Hougoumont were the gardener, Guillaume van Cutsem,[1] and his five-year-old daughter. He had meant to slip away before there was any trouble, as had so many others; but he had left it too late, and the roads were now so blocked that he decided he might as well stay.

Throughout the afternoon the 4,000 men of Major-General Cooke's 1st Division marched into their positions on the ridge

---

[1] His wife, Marie-Catherine (née Vandenplas) had left Hougoumont before the battle.

at Mont St Jean. On the left was 1st Guards Brigade, commanded by Major General Peregrine Maitland, and consisting of 2nd and 3rd Battalions of the First Guards.[2] On their right was 2nd Guards Brigade, commanded by Major-General Sir John Byng, and consisting of 2nd Battalion Coldstream Guards and 2nd Battalion Third Guards.[3]

Everyone was extremely tired, having been marching and fighting almost non-stop for the last two days in sweltering heat. They had also been soaked through in the thunderstorm that afternoon, and now thankfully threw off their heavy packs to snatch a moment's rest. But about the time they arrived at Mont St Jean another heavy thunderstorm burst on them, and in no time every man was again wet through and sloshing around in deep, sticky mud.

The few veterans there from the Peninsular War philosophically recalled that there had been just such a storm the night before the Battle of Salamanca on 22 July, 1812, and that Wellington had then won a great victory over the French the next day. They drew some comfort from the hope that their present misery might perhaps be a good omen for the morrow, but most of the officers and men simply thought of finding what little comfort they could along the windswept ridge.

One of the officers wrote of the storm, somewhat dramatically, 'Heaven's artillery, accompanied by vivid flashes of lightning, pealed in solemn and awful grandeur, while rain, pouring down in torrents, imparted the utmost gloom and discomfort to the bivouacks.'

The whole army was not only wet and cold, but also very hungry, for they had received no rations that day. Earlier that morning, while still at Quatre Bras, Colonel Francis Hepburn, Commanding Officer of 2nd Battalion Third Guards, asked one of his officers, Ensign David Baird, whether he perhaps had anything to eat that he could spare. A search of the young officer's haversack produced one Bologna sausage which they

[2] Now the Grenadier Guards.
[3] Now the Scots Guards.

26

shared, and that was all they would have until the end of the great battle the next evening.

Then at about 7 pm, just as everyone was settling down, came the decidedly unwelcome order that the four light companies of both 1st and 2nd Guards Brigades[4] were to move forward immediately and occupy the château, farm and orchard of Hougoumont in the hollow some 500 yards in front of their position midway between the Allied and French lines. Those of 1st Guards Brigade were to occupy the orchard, while those of 2nd Guards Brigade were to hold the buildings and garden of Hougoumont itself.

The light companies had been the last troops to arrive on the position at Mont St Jean, as they had been part of the rearguard under Lord Uxbridge during the withdrawal from Quatre Bras. They were looking forward to some rest; but it was not to be, and they now set off into the driving rain with the prospect of a sleepless night ahead.

One of the leading figures in our story is Private Matthew Clay[5] of the Third Guards, who survived the battle and then wrote his personal account of his experiences. He describes how he moved forward towards Hougoumont, and tried to jump across a deep, water-filled ditch. 'But the slimy ground and the increased weight of my wet blanket made me slip, and being neck-deep in the ditch, I found it very difficult to get out.'

The two light companies from 1st Guards Brigade (from 2nd and 3rd Battalions, First Guards) occupied the front edge of

[4] Each infantry battalion of the British Army consisted at full strength of six to ten companies, each up to 100 strong. One of them was a 'light company', which consisted of picked men trained as mobile troops and skirmishers, operating either as a company within their own battalion, or amalgamated to form a light battalion. Each battalion also had a 'grenadier company', again consisting of picked men. Originally the grenadiers were trained as assault troops, but by 1815 they were selected from the steadiest, most experienced men in a battalion.

[5] The men of the Guards Regiment were known as 'Privates' until they were given the title of 'Guardsmen' in 1919 by King George V, in recognition of their achievements in the First World War.

the orchard. (See page 11.) They were under the command of Lieutenant-Colonel Lord Saltoun[6] of the First Guards, who was only 30, but had already seen considerable service in Walcheren and the Peninsular War. He was renowned for his courage and initiative, and would display plenty of both during the forthcoming battle. Indeed he was later described by Wellington as 'a pattern to the army; both as man and soldier'.[7]

The farm and château were occupied by the light company of 2nd Battalion Coldstream Guards, commanded by Lieutenant-Colonel Henry Wyndham. The garden and the ground round the farm, including the lane to the west of the Great Barn, were held by the light company of 2nd Battalion Third Guards, under Lieutenant-Colonel Charles Dashwood.

In addition to the Guards, Wellington may also have sent into Hougoumont some Nassau pioneers, who would have been very useful in improving the defences.

All the troops in and around Hougoumont, except those in the orchard, were under the command of Lieutenant-Colonel James Macdonell[8] of the Coldstream Guards. He, like Saltoun, was renowned for his bravery, having won a gold medal for distinguished conduct at Maida in 1806, and he would certainly distinguish himself again at Waterloo. So the defence of Hougoumont was in good hands.

The light companies managed to occupy their positions without opposition from the French, but they were only just in time. Napoleon had also appreciated the importance of occupying Hougoumont, and, almost as soon as the Guards had moved into the buildings, some French cavalry appeared, hoping to seize the farm, but they were just too late and were sent packing with a few volleys.

---

[6] Officers in the Household Cavalry and Foot Guards at this time held 'double rank'. Thus, Lieutenants were also Captains and Captains were also Lieutenant-Colonels, which gave them seniority over officers of similar rank in other regiments.

[7] He eventually became a Field-Marshal. His name is pronounced 'Salton'.

[8] There are variations of both spelling and pronunciation.

Soon after dark an enemy foot patrol approached from the direction of the wood, but was also driven off. Colonel Macdonell decided, however, that some extra protection was required and sent a picquet from the Third Guards forward into the wood.[9] It was commanded by Captain George Evelyn and Ensign George Standen,[10] and remained there all night.

The remainder of the garrison in the farm buildings may well have thought that they would be able to enjoy a comfortable night under cover, but they were soon disillusioned, for they were immediately put to work improving the defences in every way possible. Loop-holes were made in the walls and firesteps constructed; all the entrances were closed and, if possible, barricaded.

The North, or Great Gate was deliberately left open, so that reinforcements, ammunition and supplies could reach the farm from the main position behind.

Work on improving the defences went on throughout the night and there was little sleep for anyone. There was, however, no further fighting, although the enemy could be heard a mere 300 yards away in the valley beyond the wood. The violent storm and heavy rain continued unabated, and the 15,000 men of Reille's corps probably suffered rather more than the 500 or so men of the Guards in and around Hougoumont.

Those in Hougoumont were certainly better off than their comrades in the main position on the ridge. Ensign Charles Lake of the Third Guards described his miserable night:

'The rain was incessant during the night and I shall never forget my Friend, the Honble Captain Forbes, (whose servant had forgotten his cloak) asking for a corner of my large one to lay under. Poor fellow! It was his last sleep for he was shot through the breast early on the morning of the

[9] Reports differ as to whether it was right forward 'on the *South* edge' (which would have been extremely close to the French positions), or whether it was on the *North* edge of the wood, quite close to the farm, which seems more likely.

[10] He, like Private Clay, left us an account of events at Hougoumont.

eighteenth, and hereby hangs a romantic tale, he being struck on that part of the breast on which hung the miniature of the lady to whom he was engaged, and with whom I have often seen him dance at the Brussels balls.

During the night our General (Byng) slept close to us, covered with nothing but straw, and bellowed lustily at one of our officers accidentally treading on him.'

Ensign Charles Short of the Coldstream, aged only $16\frac{1}{2}$, had an equally uncomfortable time:

'We were under arms the whole night expecting the attack and it rained to that degree that the field where we were was half-way up our legs in mud; nobody, of course, could lie down. The ague got hold of some of the men. I with another officer had a blanket and with a little more gin we kept up very well. We had only one fire, and you cannot conceive the state we were in. We formed a hollow square and prepared to receive Cavalry twice, but found it was a false alarm both times.

Soon after daylight the Commissary sent up with the greatest difficulty some gin and we found an old cask full of wet rye loaves which we breakfasted upon. Everyone was in high spirits.'

Dawn, when it came at last, was a welcome sight to both sides, even though it was still raining. The 68,000 Allied troops along the Mont St Jean ridge woke, cold, wet and hungry, and looked across the waterlogged valley at the 72,000 equally sodden and miserable French on the other side.

Ten miles to the east, at Wavre, 30,000 Prussians were just setting out to march to Wellington's support, as Marshal Blücher had promised they would.

The stage was set.

Chapter 5
'Ah. But You Do Not Know Macdonell'

Dawn, 18 June, 1815

Just before dawn on Sunday,[1] 18 June, the troops in and around
Hougoumont all 'stood to', ready for the French attack that
might come at any moment. The rain was still falling, and it was
a miserable, muddy awakening.

Lord Saltoun was in the orchard with his two light companies
when a staff officer appeared, at the head of a battalion of Nassau
infantry, (about 600 strong),[2] a company of 300 Hanoverian
Jäger (sharp-shooters),[3] and also about 100 picked Luneberg
infantry.[4] He told Saltoun that he was to hand over responsibility
for the defence of the orchard to this new force and was then to
rejoin 1st Guards Brigade.

Saltoun duly handed over and was half-way back to his original position on the ridge when he met the Duke of Wellington,
accompanied by his Military Secretary, Lieutenant-Colonel
Lord Fitzroy Somerset of the First Guards.

The Duke called out, 'Hallo. Who are you? Where are you
going?'

Saltoun halted and, ordering his men to lie down and rest, he
then explained the orders he had received. The Duke seemed

---

[1] Other great battles that took place on a Sunday were Blenheim (1704), Badajoz
(1812), Inkerman (1854) and the Gallipoli landings in 1915.
[2] The 1st Battalion of the 2nd Nassau Brigade in Papelotte, commanded by
Major Büssen.
[3] No 1 Company from Count Kielmansegge's 1st Hanoverian Brigade.
[4] From Count Kielmansegge's Jäger Corps.

31

surprised and replied, 'Well, I was not aware of such an order. However, don't join the brigade yet. Remain quiet where you are until further orders from me.'

As the Duke rode on, he remarked to an aide, 'That was one of my old Peninsular officers. See how he made his men lie down.'

Wellington then made his way towards Hougoumont. He was dressed in a blue civilian coat,[5] white buckskins, Hessian boots, a white cravat and a blue cloak, (which he frequently put on when there were showers). His cocked hat[6] carried no plume, but four cockades – to represent England, Spain, Portugal and the Netherlands. It was an unobtrusive uniform, and it may in fact have contributed to his survival that day, particularly just after his meeting with Saltoun.

Following his usual practice of seeing everything for himself and making quite sure that his orders had been carried out, Wellington made his way down the slope to the orchard, and then across it to the wood. It was a rash thing to do, with the French so close,[7] and it so happened that, as he halted on the track leading towards La Belle Alliance, a French tirailleur (skirmisher) was hidden in the undergrowth a mere 10 yards from him.

Fortunately the man did not recognize what an important target he had within range at that moment and did not even fire. He thus missed his chance of altering history and earning his own place in the history books.

It is not certain on which of his visits to Hougoumont that Wellington ordered the Nassauers and Hanoverians into the wood, but it seems probable that it was on this occasion, in order to forestall the French in seizing it. Whatever the precise time, the Nassauers, Lunebergers and Hanoverians moved forward

[5] The civilian coat led some contemporary accounts to describe him incorrectly as wearing civilian dress.
[6] Wellington wore his cocked hat 'fore and aft', whereas Napoleon wore his 'four-square'.
[7] Wellington came close to being captured on three occasions in the Peninsular War.

early that morning into the wood, which they occupied without opposition.

At the same time Wellington ordered part of the light company of the Third Guards to be moved from the garden of Hougoumont (which was now protected by the troops in the wood) and take up a new position round the track junction by the haystack at the south-west corner of the farm.[8]

This divided the defences at Hougoumont into three sectors. The first was the orchard, held by the light companies of the First Guards under Saltoun. Then came the garden and the buildings, which were held by the Coldstream light company, while the Third Guards company was responsible for the lane to the west of the farm. Colonel Macdonell remained in command of the two latter sectors.

Meanwhile, work continued non-stop on the fortification of the buildings, and more loop-holes were made in the garden walls. This was to be an important factor later in the holding of the position.

Before the Battle

While the soldiers, both Allied and French, could do little but wait for orders, the two commanders had much to think about, and each was planning possible moves in the bloody conflict that they knew must soon take place.

Fortunately for the Allies, Napoleon saw no particular reason to hurry, and he breakfasted at Le Caillou around 8 am. 'Tonight we will sleep in Brussels,' he declared, and ordered 'a well-done shoulder of lamb' for supper that evening.

At about 9 in the morning he summoned a conference at Le Caillou to issue his orders for the battle. Rather surprisingly he decided that he would not launch his main attack until 1 pm, so as to give time for the ground to dry out, which would make his artillery more effective. It was a major error, for it gave the

[8] It is intriguing that the site of the haystack at Hougoumont today is still in much the same spot.

Prussians that much more time to reach Wellington.

In order to keep the enemy occupied in the meantime he ordered Reille's Corps to attack Hougoumont. He anticipated no difficulty over this operation, which he regarded as 'just a diversion'; he hoped it would also make Wellington move troops from his centre to reinforce his right flank, and so weaken his centre before the main French assault.

Reille in turn gave the task of carrying out this 'diversion' to Napoleon's brother, Prince Jerome, with his 6th Division of 6,000 men supported by General Piré's 2nd Cavalry Division. 'It is simply a question,' he told Jerome, 'of keeping in the hollow behind the wood in support of a strong line of skirmishers in front.' In fact it turned out to be a very different story.

At around this time the rain eased at long last and 140,000 men tried to dry themselves out in the ankle-deep mud and the sodden, trampled crops. A crackle of musket fire came from both sides of the valley as soldiers fired their weapons to clear them of mud and damp. The Commissariat winced at the waste of ammunition, but it was the simplest way of ensuring that a musket was in working order, and a man's life might depend on just that.

Although the two sides were within sight of each other, no shots had yet been fired in anger, and the two armies each went about their own business, preparing for the confrontation that could not now be far off.

At 10 am those Allied soldiers in sight of the French watched in wonder as Napoleon on his white mare Désirée reviewed his Grand Armée in front of La Belle Alliance. It was a magnificent sight that stirred the emotions of the French and raised their spirits still higher. Cheers and shouts of 'Vive L'Empereur' reached across the valley, but they did not worry the phlegmatic British troops, who were more concerned now to get the battle over and done with.

Wellington, on the other hand, looked on every minute of delay as a welcome bonus, in that it gave more time for the Prussians to appear. Seeing that Napoleon was evidently not about to attack for a while yet, he made his way once again down to Hougoumont to make absolutely sure that everything there was being done as he required.

It was shortly before 11 am when he rode down to the château, accompanied this time by his Prussian Liaison Officer, General Müffling. They met Macdonell, and Wellington warned him that he must expect to be attacked before long. He again stressed the vital importance of holding Hougoumont and gave orders that the garrison must 'defend the post to the last extremity'.

Müffling, who liked to discuss tactics with the Duke, questioned whether the place really could be held, seeing how exposed it was and how few men, a mere 1,500 or so, had been allocated to its defence.

'Ah,' replied the Duke, 'but you do not know Macdonell.'

Chapter 6
'Here They Come, Boys'

The First French Attack

Considering how much has been written about the Battle of Waterloo, (or perhaps because of it!) it is strange that it is still not certain when the first shot was fired in anger on 18 June, 1815. Various individuals who were there gave times ranging from 10 am to midday, but the likeliest answer seems to be that it was around 11.30, when Prince Jerome launched his first attack against Hougoumont.

As ordered, he began by sending a strong line of skirmishers into the wood from the valley where they had spent the night. They had some 300 yards of thick wood and undergrowth to clear, and, in the face of stiff resistance by the Nassauers and Hanoverians, they made slow progress.

As always, Wellington was soon at the scene of action and he promptly ordered up two batteries of guns,[1] which he positioned on the ridge behind Hougoumont, from where they gave good covering fire on to the wood and the open ground round it.

The French assault soon developed into a full-scale attack, with Bauduin's Brigade advancing through the wood from the south. They were supported by the light cavalry of Piré's 2nd Cavalry Division, who attacked to the west of the Nivelles road.

Fierce fighting went on for about half an hour, in the course of which Bauduin was killed. But the Nassauers and Hano-

---

[1] Captain Sandham's Battery attached to 1st Division, and Captain Cleeve's Battery attached to the K.G.L.

1 The Coldstream Guards outside the South Gate. A painting by D. Dighton. By courtesy of the Trustees of the National Army Museum.

verians were driven steadily back out of the wood and were forced to take up new positions along the south edge of the orchard, where the First Guards had been during the night.

Wellington had meantime brought up Major Bull's Battery of six 5½-inch howitzers, and they came into action on his direct orders. They opened fire on the wood, over the heads of the Allied troops, and this was so effective that Wellington commented in his Despatches on 'this service which, considering the proximity of the Allied troops in the Coppice, was of a very delicate nature, executed with admirable skill and attended with the desired effect.'[2]

---

[2] The French officer leading these troops stated later that the first salvo killed seventeen men.

Nevertheless, by about midday the French had reached the north edge of the wood and found themselves within sight of Hougoumont. Siborne describes the scene:

'In the full confidence that this important post was now within their grasp, they rushed forward at the *"pas de charge"* to force an entrance. A deadly fire bursting forth from the loopholes and platforms along the garden wall, which was parallel to and about thirty yards distance from the hedge, laid prostrate the leading files. Those who came up in rapid succession were staggered by the sudden and unexpected appearance of this little fortress!'

Every shot from the Guards behind the loopholed walls found a target among the French, who could in return only fire at a virtually invisible enemy. Some French soldiers tried to break down the solid South Gate with the butts of their muskets, but were soon shot down; others tried to climb over the garden wall, but were promptly bayoneted.

The attack made no progress at all, but to the east the Nassauers and Hanoverians, having withdrawn from the wood, were steadily driven back across the orchard to the Hollow Way.

At about the time of the first French attack, the light companies of the First Guards under Saltoun had been ordered to move back from the spot where Wellington had told them to stay. They had just joined their battalions for a welcome rest, when a shout went up: 'The Nassauers are driven out of the orchard. Light companies to the front.'

They immediately formed up and moved forward down the hill. They once more met the Duke, who sent them on their way with the words: 'In with you, my lads, and let me see no more of you.'

When they reached the Hollow Way they charged the French and drove them back across the orchard and on into the wood.

2 A French Attack against the South Gate. A painting by
  E. Croft. By courtesy of Christopher D'Ambrumenil.

They then re-occupied the defences that they had held previously along the south edge of the orchard, but they found to their disgust that 'all the preparations they had made for defence [had been] completely destroyed, and during the action they had to trust to sheer hard fighting, often hand to hand, to maintain their ground.'

For the moment the situation at Hougoumont was stabilized. The French had lost some 1,500 men in their first attack and the Allied garrison was still holding out.

Wellington now withdrew the weary Nassau battalion and brought forward Du Plat's Brigade to strengthen the reserve on the ridge behind Hougoumont.

The Second French Attack

Prince Jerome might well have 'called it a day' at this point, on the basis that he had fully carried out the Emperor's orders to create a diversion at Hougoumont. Indeed, both Marshal Reille and his own Chief of Staff, advised him that he had done enough and should not commit more troops to the operation.

But Jerome was determined to prove himself and was not pleased that he had failed to take Hougoumont.[3] He therefore set about mounting another attack, this time primarily from the west rather than the south.[4] Soye's Brigade replaced the weakened brigade of the late Bauduin, with orders to attack once more from the wood. Jerome meanwhile would attack the west side of the farm, while Piré's light cavalry were to swing round and come in on Hougoumont from the north.

It was a good plan and it came very close to success, being thwarted only by the famous Closing of the Gates.

---

[3] In his defence it should be recorded that, in a conversation several years later, he maintained that Napoleon said to him *about an hour after the battle began*, 'If Grouchy does not come up or if you do not carry Hougoumont, the battle is decidedly lost – so go – go and carry Hougoumont – *coûte que coûte.*' If true, this not only explains but also justifies his actions.

[4] See map on page 11.

Chapter 7
Closing the Gates

The time was now around midday and the situation was that the orchard was firmly held by the two light companies of the First Guards and the Hanoverians under Saltoun, while the buildings and garden of Hougoumont were equally firmly held by the light companies of the Coldstream and Third Guards under Macdonell.

The light company of the Third Guards, under Lieutenant-Colonel Charles Dashwood, was at this time positioned outside the farm on the south-west corner of the buildings. This detachment, numbering less than 100 men, now took the full force of the second French attack, and was steadily driven back down the lane along the west side of the farm towards the North Gate.

Sergeant Fraser and Colonel Cubières
The leading enemy infantry were the 1st Light Regiment of Bauduin's Brigade, and in the fierce hand-to-hand fighting that developed, Sergeant Ralph Fraser of the Third Guards, a Peninsular War veteran, found himself engaged in personal combat with the Commanding Officer of the 1st Light Regiment, Colonel Cubières.

The Colonel slashed at him with his sword, but Sergeant Fraser defended himself with his halberd, and then used it to pull the Colonel off his horse. Leaving him lying on the ground, Sergeant Fraser leapt onto the horse and galloped triumphantly back to the North Gate. There he joined his comrades who were by now withdrawing back to the small orchard.

Colonel Cubières was wounded, but he survived, and later

became a general and Governor of Ancona, in Italy. In 1832 he met Colonel Alexander Woodford of the Coldstream Guards, who was also at Hougoumont (see page 47) and they naturally started talking about the battle. According to Woodford, Cubières declared that when he lay wounded 'the Guards forebore to fire on him, and he owed us much for many good years since'.

Private Clay

Another man who was lucky to survive this battle outside Hougoumont was our friend Private Matthew Clay of the Third Guards. He was only 20 years old and in the smoke and confusion, he found himself left behind when the rest of the light company retreated towards the Great Gate. With him was his comrade, Private Gann aged 41, whom he described as 'My senior by some years and a very steady, undaunted old soldier'.

Clay wrote of their ordeal:

> 'We were earnestly engaged [by the enemy] ... we were now left to ourselves and could see no one near us. The enemy skirmishers remained under cover and continued firing at us, and we fired back and retired down the road up which we had advanced. My musket now proving defective was very discouraging, but looking on the ground I saw a musket ... which was warm from use and proved an excellent one. ... On turning my eyes to the lower gates (Great Gate) I saw they were open ... and we hurried towards them. On entering the courtyard I saw the doors, or rather the gates, were riddled with shot holes. In the entrance lay many dead bodies of the enemy.'

Clay must have been one of the last of the Guards from outside Hougoumont to withdraw through the open gate and, as soon as he was safely inside, an attempt was made to shut it against the pursuing French troops.

Closing the Gates

Some men of the Light Regiment, however, rushed forward and made a determined effort to break in through the half-open gate. At their head was a giant of a man called Lieutenant Legros, appropriately known as *L'Enfonceur*, or the Smasher. Seizing an axe from one of the pioneers, he swung it against the panels of the gate and forced his way into the farmyard.

A number of Frenchmen[1] surged forward behind him, and it must have seemed to them for a moment that the capture of Hougoumont was in sight. Desperate close-quarter fighting developed on all sides, with French and British struggling hand-

---

[1] Some accounts say as many as 100 entered the courtyard but it was probably nearer 30 or 40.

to-hand in the farmyard.

Some of the enemy reached as far as the château, but they all came under intense fire from the château windows, as well as from the buildings on all sides. One group pursued a Hanoverian officer called Lieutenant Wilder as far as the farmer's house, and as he grasped the handle of a door to open it a French sapeur cut off his hand with an axe.

But the French were heavily out-numbered and had little chance. Before long every one of them was killed or wounded except for one unarmed drummer-boy, who was spared. *L'Enfonceur* himself died near the château, his axe still grasped in his hand.

But even as the fighting was taking place inside Hougoumont, more French were trying to force their way in through the gate. Lieutenant-Colonel Macdonell was by the Garden Gate when he became aware of the danger, and at once realized that it was vital that the Great Gate be closed. Shouting to three other Coldstream Guards officers nearby[2] to join him, he rushed towards the gate.

As the four of them reached the area of the draw-well, they were joined by two more Coldstreamers[3] and four men from the Third Guards.[4] Thrusting their way forward, the group of ten drove back any enemy in their way and fought their way to the gate. Colonel Macdonell, who was a large, strong man, put his

[2] Lieutenant-Colonel Henry Wyndham.
  Ensign James Hervey.
  Ensign Henry Gooch.
[3] *Coldstream Guards.*
  Corporal James Graham (he was promoted to Sergeant after the battle).
  Corporal Joseph Graham (his brother).
[4] *Third Guards.*
  Sergeant Ralph Fraser.
  Sergeant Bruce McGregor.
  Sergeant Joseph Aston.
  Private Joseph Lester.
  There are varying versions of some of these names.

4 After the Closing of the Gates. A painting by J. Crofts, 1891. By courtesy of the Cavalry and Guards Club.

shoulder to it, together with Corporal James Graham, who was also of heavy build. Others joined in, either adding their weight to the gates or thrusting back the Frenchmen who were still trying to force their way in.

Very slowly the two heavy panels were pushed together, and held in position until they could be barricaded. There was a rush to collect any timbers or other pieces of debris that could be used to reinforce the gate, and finally the massive crossbar was dropped into position.

So the gates at Hougoumont were closed, but it had been a 'near-run thing'.

The struggle was not yet over, however. Even while the gate was being secured, some of the enemy tried to scale the walls, and one French Grenadier, standing on the shoulders of a comrade, leaned over the top and took aim at Colonel Wyndham.[5] Fortunately Wyndham saw him out of the corner of his eye; he hurriedly handed a musket to Corporal Graham beside him, who fired at the same second as the Frenchman – and it was the latter who fell back, shot in the brain.

So the Great Gate was closed, and was never again forced by the enemy. Nor indeed did any enemy penetrate into Hougoumont for the rest of the day, and it is not hard to see why Wellington later declared that 'The success of the Battle of Waterloo turned on the closing of the gates [at Hougoumont]'.

[5] His niece said of him that because of Hougoumont he would never thereafter for the rest of his life close any door, as a result often sitting in a howling draught for hours on end.

Chapter 8
Attack and Counter-Attack

Counter-Attack by the Coldstream Guards

Major-General Byng, commanding 2nd Guards Brigade, had been keeping a close watch on the fighting at Hougoumont, and when he saw the mêlée round the North Gate, he ordered the remainder of 2nd Battalion Coldstream Guards to move forward and counter-attack the French who had penetrated round to the north side of Hougoumont.

The battalion was commanded by Lieutenant-Colonel Alexander Woodford, a Peninsular War veteran who would later become a Field-Marshal.

Three Coldstream companies[1] reached the North Gate soon after it had been finally closed by Colonel Macdonell and, after some stiff fighting, they drove the French back down the lane and then into the wood.

'We found the enemy very near the wall,' Colonel Woodford recorded later, 'and charged them, upon which they went off, and I took the opportunity of entering the farm by a side door in the lane' (the West Door).

The remainder of the battalion (less two companies left on the ridge with the Colours)[2] then moved into the farm.

Colonel Woodford was in fact now the senior officer in Hou-

[1] Grenadier Company.   Lieutenant-Colonel D. MacKinnon.
No 1 Company.   Lieutenant-Colonel T. Sowerby
No 4 Company.   Lieutenant-Colonel The Hon E. Acheson
[2] Nos 7 & 8 Companies. The officers of these companies, however, left the Colours in the care of the Non-Commissioned Officers and themselves joined in the fighting in Hougoumont.

47

goumont, but he generously declined to take over command from Colonel Macdonell, who was doing so well, and they fought the battle together for the rest of the day.

The 600 or so additional Coldstreamers made a welcome reinforcement for the hard-pressed light companies inside Hougoumont and in particular their arrival made it possible for Macdonell to strengthen the defences along the east wall of the garden, which enfiladed the orchard; this was a move that would pay excellent dividends later on, and would help to repulse several attacks on the orchard.

Soon after the Coldstreamers had taken up their positions inside the farm there were several sporadic French attacks from the direction of the wood, but they were beaten off without difficulty, and for a while there was a lull in the fighting.

The Third French Attack[3]

Despite the failure of his second attack, Jerome was undeterred, and at about 12.45 he launched a third assault, directed this time against the south-east side of the orchard. This was more serious from the Allied point of view, as there was a danger that, if successful, the French might be able to swing round behind Hougoumont and so isolate it from the main position.

This third French attack involved Foy's Division from Reille's Corps, and was led by Gautier's Brigade. As they advanced towards the orchard they were watched by General Sir Charles Alten, commanding the 3rd Division, who soon appreciated the threat that this attack posed. He prepared to send in his light companies to counter it, but was restrained by his corps commander, the Prince of Orange, who told him: 'No. Don't move. The Duke is sure to see the movement and will take some steps to counter it.'

Sure enough, at around 1 pm, help did come, though it is more likely that it was initiated by Major-General Byng, commanding

---

[3] See map on page 11.

48

2nd Guards Brigade. He sent forward two companies of the Third Guards[4] under Lieutenant-Colonel Francis Home to counter the advancing French.

It proved most successful, and they not only halted the enemy who were out-flanking the Allied defences in the orchard, but they also drove them back.

At the same time the Coldstream lining the garden wall of the château opened a deadly fire on the enemy in the orchard, and the French attack crumbled. Saltoun and his light companies again advanced and re-occupied the orchard; so the third French attack on Hougoumont had failed.

Meanwhile the main battle was now about to begin, and at 1 pm some eighty French guns intensified their fire on the Allied left, where Napoleon was ready to launch his thrust for Brussels.

Forty-five minutes later the bombardment ceased and the four divisons of D'Erlon's Corps advanced confidently across the fields to the east of the main road. It was an awesome sight, 16,000 infantry in columns 200 files across and 24 deep, but, as is well known, they were repulsed with some 7,000 casualties and the loss of two Eagles.

Meanwhile, the 'battle within a battle' continued at Hougoumont throughout the afternoon with the French making a series of uncoordinated attacks, primarily against the orchard. It is difficult to present a clear picture of events and identify each attack and counter-attack. Some accounts tell of only *three* French attacks; others refer to some *seven* actions at Hougoumont during the day.

The Fourth French Attack

The French now brought up a howitzer, which began to shell the buildings of Hougoumont. It was positioned in the northeast corner of the wood, and Lord Saltoun decided that it must be captured or at least silenced.

[4] The Grenadier Company and No 1 Company.

49

He strengthened his own exhausted light companies with the Grenadier Company of the Third Guards and fifty Hanoverians and charged into the wood. But he found himself opposed by the best part of three French brigades, and it was an impossible task. He was eventually driven back across the orchard and into the Hollow Way once again.

The light companies of the First Guards had now been fighting almost non-stop since 11 o'clock and orders came for them to return to their battalions in 1st Guards Brigade, who had not as yet been engaged. Saltoun 'returned to his battalion with about one third of the men with whom he had gone into action.' He himself had had four horses shot under him during the day, but amazingly was unhurt.

Saltoun's men were replaced in the Hollow Way by the remainder of 2nd Battalion Third Guards[5] under Colonel Francis Hepburn, who would be in command of that sector for the rest of the day.[6]

He soon decided that the first task must be to regain possession of the orchard. 'After a little pause,' he recalled, 'we advanced upon the enemy, crossed the orchard and occupied the front hedge, which I considered my post.'

Once the attack by D'Erlon's Corps had been repulsed, there was a brief lull and Wellington took the opportunity to make some adjustments to his right flank in order to fill the gaps caused by the commitment of the whole of 2nd Guards Brigade to the defence of Hougoumont. He moved Hew Halkett's 3rd Hanoverian Brigade up on the left of Du Plat's Brigade, which he had moved forward earlier, and so effectively replaced 2nd Guards Brigade in the line. He also shifted Mitchell's Brigade slightly to its left, so that it was more directly behind Hougoumont.[7]

At the same time the Duke moved the whole Brunswick Corps

---

[5] The companies concerned were Nos 6, 7 and 8. They left their Colours on the main position.

[6] Colonel Hepburn said that he moved 'As near as I can judge, about one o'clock'. But it seems more likely that it was in fact nearer two o'clock.

[7] See map on page 22.

forward from Merbe Braine and positioned five battalions from it behind Maitland's 1st Guards Brigade. He also sent one Brunswick battalion into Hougoumont to reinforce the garrison, and two K.G.L. battalions to support the Third Guards in the Orchard.

With three new battalions now in support of Hougoumont, there were some 2,000 troops involved in its defence, and Wellington had, in addition, reinforced the right of his line by about 4,000 men. But he had not in the process weakened his centre, as Napoleon had hoped he would; instead, he had found the extra troops required from his right flank, having decided that Napoleon was no longer likely to attack him there in strength.

The French, on the other hand, had committed to the 'diversion' at Hougoumont at least 8,000 men who were badly needed elsewhere.

The Fifth French Attack[8]

Some time between 2 and 3 pm the fifth French attack was made against Hougoumont. This time it was carried out by a new division, that of General Bachelu, and it came from the direction of La Belle Alliance, that is from the south-east.

This line of approach meant that the advancing French columns had to march diagonally across the Allied front, and in the process they were exposed to such intense artillery fire, particularly from Captain Cleeve's K.G.L. Battery, that the attack was broken up before it ever reached the orchard.

For a brief moment there was a lull in the fighting round Hougoumont, and the weary troops there could, for a while, watch the rest of the Allied Army take up the struggle.

Colonel Hepburn
At about 4 pm[9] General Cooke, commanding 1st Division, was severely wounded and was replaced by Major-General Byng

[8] See map on page 11.
[9] This is according to General Byng himself, though others (Siborne (435) and the Coldstream Guards History) say it was earlier.

51

from 2nd Guards Brigade; he in turn was replaced by Colonel Hepburn, the Commanding Officer of the Third Guards. This was appropriate, in that the whole of 2nd Guards Brigade was by now engaged in and around Hougoumont, where Colonel Hepburn himself was positioned. But he faced a considerable responsibility and a difficult task that included trying to maintain communications not only with 1st Division but also with Macdonell under siege in Hougoumont.

The garrison in Hougoumont now consisted of eight companies of 2nd Battalion of the Coldstream Guards, together with the light company of the Third Guards, and a Brunswick Battalion. The orchard was held by 2nd Battalion of the Third Guards, and some fifty Hanoverians, with two K.G.L. battalions in support; so there must have been over 4,000 men now involved in the defence of Hougoumont.

'Of all these I had command,' Colonel Hepburn wrote later, 'and was not idle.'

For the rest of the day, some four hours out of nine,[10] Colonel Hepburn would, as Brigade Commander, be responsible for all the fighting round Hougoumont. Yet when Wellington came to write his Despatch, he mentioned Colonels Macdonell and Home as being responsible for the defence of Hougoumont, but made no mention at all of Colonel Hepburn.

Wellington admitted later to General Byng that he regretted the omission, but he refused to rectify it publicly, declaring that he 'never altered a Despatch'.[11]

---

[10] Siborne (435) says that Hepburn took over at 2 pm and so was in command for six hours out of nine.

[11] Colonel Hepburn was not alone in failing to receive due recognition publicly from the Duke. Colonel Colborne, commanding the 52nd (Oxfordshire Light Infantry) at Waterloo, distinguished himself by manoeuvring his battalion brilliantly during the attack by the Imperial Guard, and so contributing decisively to their repulse, but he likewise received no mention in Wellington's Despatch.

It is said that Wellington was asked many years later what he might have done differently if he had his life over again, and he is alleged to have replied, 'I should have given more praise'. (Diary of Edmund Wheatley, p. 69).

Chapter 9
'I See That the Fire has Spread'

As the afternoon progressed Napoleon realized that some new initiative was called for if he was to gain Hougoumont, and at around 2.45pm he ordered up a battery of howitzers to shell the buildings. They fired 'carcass' projectiles,[1] which soon set fire to the thatched roofs of the farm. By 3pm the château, the chapel and the Great Barn were all ablaze.

Doubtless Napoleon thought that the fire would drive out the defenders, where his troops had failed, but he was proved wrong.[2]

'The heat and smoke of the conflagration were very difficult to bear,' wrote Colonel Woodford. 'Several men were burnt as neither Colonel Macdonell or myself could penetrate to the stables where the wounded had been carried.'

At this moment Corporal James Graham of the Coldstream, who had helped to close the gate, approached Colonel Macdonell and asked permission to leave his post in the firing line in the garden. Well aware of Graham's bravery, the Colonel queried why he wanted to retire at such a critical moment.

'I would not,' replied the Corporal. 'Only my brother lies wounded in that building which has just caught fire.'

Permission was given, and his brother Joseph (who had also been involved in the closing of the gates) was removed to safety,

[1] They contained an incendiary device within the shell and were designed to set fire to any target.
[2] It was one of Napoleon's mistakes at Waterloo that he did not use his artillery earlier against Hougoumont. Firing solid shot, they would probably have made a breach in the walls and so enabled his infantry to get inside the buildings.

whereupon Corporal Graham immediately returned to his post.

There were wounded from both sides in all the buildings, including the chapel, which was now on fire. There are several eye-witness accounts of how the flames licked through the doorway of the chapel and set fire to the feet of the life-size wooden statue of Christ on the Cross which hung just above the door. But they then stopped, miraculously it seemed to some, leaving the feet charred and black, but the remainder of the body untouched.

Ensign George Standen of the Third Guards wrote home: 'The anecdote of the fire only burning to the feet of the Cross is perfectly true, which in so superstitious a country made a great sensation.' The figure is still there today, though on a side wall, and one can see that, although the feet are badly charred, the remainder of the figure is untouched.

The same officer also described how 'three or four officers' horses rushed out into the yard from the barn and in a minute or two rushed back into the flames and were burnt'.

The fire had meanwhile been noticed by Wellington, who immediately wrote a message reinforcing his original orders that Hougoumont must be held at all costs. It was written, as was his custom, in his own hand on a slip of ass's skin[3], because that provided a smooth surface that was largely waterproof and could be wiped clean (an early version of talc!). The message read:

> 'I see that the fire has communicated from the Hay Stack to the Roof of the château. You must however still keep your men in those parts to which the fire does not reach. Take care that no men are lost by the falling-in of the Roof or Floors. After they have both fallen in, occupy the ruined walls inside of the Garden; particularly if it should be possible for the enemy to pass through the Embers in the inside of the House.'

The Duke's remarkably detailed orders were carried down to Hougoumont by Major Andrew Hamilton, one of the ADCs to

[3] The original is in Apsley House and is one of only four to survive.

5 Wellington's Message about the Fire. By courtesy of the Trustees of the Wellington Museum, Apsley House.

Major-General Sir Edward Barnes, who was Adjutant General to the Forces. They were delivered by him to Colonel Home of the Third Guards.

Having delivered his message, Major Hamilton rode off, but returned shortly afterwards to ask if Colonel Home had perfectly understood the orders.

'I do,' replied the Colonel, 'and you can tell the Duke from me that unless we are attacked more vigorously than we have been hitherto, we shall maintain the position without difficulty.'

Shortly afterwards Colonel Home entered the buildings, found Colonel Woodford and Colonel Macdonell, and passed on the Duke's orders to them.

Most of Hougoumont was by now burning fiercely and there was nothing that could be done to quell the blaze. It must have been a particularly horrifying ordeal for the wounded, some of whom crawled out of the buildings with their uniforms alight.

It was not much better for those who were still fighting. Burning timbers crashed down on them as they manned their positions. Thick, choking smoke billowed everywhere, making their eyes stream as they strained through the dense smog, watching for the next enemy assault; red-hot, flying sparks burned their uniforms and started new fires. Through the roar of the flames and the crash of falling beams came cries for help from the wounded and the wild neighing of panic-stricken horses. Enemy shells still crashed into the buildings and the musket fire was incessant.

Yet the defenders stayed at their posts and fought on.

Private Matthew Clay was in the château:

'I was told off with others under Lieutenant Gough (sic. probably Ensign Gooch) of the Coldstream Guards and was posted in an upper room. This room was situated higher than the surrounding buildings and we annoyed the enemy's skirmishers from the window. The enemy noticed this and threw their shells amongst us and set the building which we were defending on fire. Our officer placed himself at the entrance of the room and would not allow anyone to leave his post until our position became hopeless and too perilous to remain. We fully expected the floor to sink with us every moment, and in our escape several of us were more or less injured.'

So, while Hougoumont blazed and disintegrated round them the Guards remained at their posts, and not a single Frenchman managed to penetrate into either the buildings or the garden.

At some stage during the afternoon, while the fire was at its height, the gardener's daughter was apparently led out of the farm through the North Gate by a Guards Sergeant, and from there found her way safely into the Fôret de Soignes. Sixty-five years later she came to England, aged 70, on her first visit,[4] and she then described how she clearly remembered the fierce fighting at Hougoumont, and how kindly treated she was by the British Guards, who fed her scraps of their biscuits.

Enemy pressure on the approaches to Hougoumont from the north was steadily increasing and it was only with the greatest difficulty that the vital line of communication to the North Gate was kept open by the Coldstream, whose responsibility it was. It was just as well that they succeeded in this task, for there was now a crisis as supplies of ammunition began to run low.

The situation was saved by Ensign Berkeley Drummond, Acting Adjutant of the 2nd Battalion Third Guards, who was (presumably) in the orchard with Colonel Hepburn. According to Captain Horace Seymour of the Staff, who was also an A.D.C. to Lord Uxbridge, Ensign Drummond:

'called to me to use my best endeavours to send them musket ammunition. Soon afterwards I fell in with a Private of the Waggon Train in charge of a Tumbril on the crest of the position. I merely pointed out to him where he was wanted,

---

[4] She stayed with a Captain Kerrish in Gedleston, Norfolk, and her story was written up in the *Norwich Argus*. Her name then was given as Madame van Cutsem, and she was described as a widow.

when he gallantly started his horses and drove straight down to the farm, to the gate of which I saw him arrive. He must have lost his horses as there was severe fire kept on him. I feel convinced to that man's service the Guards owe their ammunition.'[5]

There is doubt as to the identity of this brave man, but it is likely that he was Private Joseph Brewer of the Royal Waggon Train. He is said to have transferred to the Third Guards after Waterloo, but neither they nor the Waggon Train can find any mention of this in their records. A mystery hero.

---

[5] *The Coldstream Guards Regimental History* states that the tumbril arrived 'about one o'clock' and 'proved most seasonable'.

Chapter 10
'Hard Pounding, Gentlemen'

'Prepare to Receive Cavalry'

The battle was steadily building up to a crisis. Napoleon knew by now that Blücher and his Prussians were within striking distance and that time was therefore no longer on his side. He now ordered Ney to take La Haye Sainte at all costs and open up the road to Brussels.

At 4pm Ney launched the first of the two great cavalry charges that the French would make that day. Over 4,500 horsemen pounded across the muddy valley and on up the slope, where the Allied troops waited. But the cavalry were not supported by either infantry or artillery, and without them they could not break the Allied squares.

Five times the French attacked and five times they were beaten off. Ensign Gronow of the First Guards described the noise of the musket balls striking the enemy's cuirasses as being like 'a violent hail-storm beating upon panes of glass.'

The Allied cavalry counter-attacked time and time again, and for over an hour the two sides charged and wheeled, cut and thrust, round the twenty defiant squares.

For over an hour the attacks went on with the utmost gallantry and determination; but even when Napoleon threw in a further 5,000 horsemen, the ever-dwindling squares still stood firm. Finally, it was the French who withdrew, with the breakthrough still not achieved.

The defence of Hougoumont can be said to have contributed to the defeat of the cavalry attacks. The fact that both Hou-

goumont and La Haye Sainte were still in Allied hands meant
that as the French cavalry charged they were under fire from
both flanks. They were therefore forced to advance on a very
restricted front of only 800 yards, thus losing some impact and
also providing a better target for the artillery. Hougoumont has
been described as 'a thorn in the side of all the French attacks',
and this was certainly true of the two cavalry charges.

It must have been a magnificent sight for the men of the Third
Guards in the orchard as they watched the mass of enemy horses
thunder past to their left, and they probably enjoyed taking a
few pot shots at them too.

Sixth French Attack[1]

But they were not to be allowed to remain mere spectators for
long. Just about the same time as the cavalry charges, two
regiments of Foy's Division, together with the remnants of
Bachelu's Division, launched yet another attack on Hougoumont, this time against the south-east of the orchard.

Despite the support of the two K.G.L. line battalions sent to
their aid, the Third Guards were heavily outnumbered and
could not hold off the French attack.

'We were warmly attacked,' reported Hepburn, 'our left
turned, and we were driven back to the Hollow Way, where we
rallied. But when the attacking troops attempted to pass through
the orchard they received so destructive a fire from the Coldstream Guards posted inside the Garden Wall, that they were
completely staggered, and we meanwhile advanced and regained
our post.'

Ensign Charles Lake of the Third Guards wrote: 'Poor
Captain Forbes ... was shot ... I was shot a wee bit above the
right temple ... Poor Sir David Baird ... a musket ball struck
him immediately above the chin and lodged in his throat ... So

[1] See map on page 11.

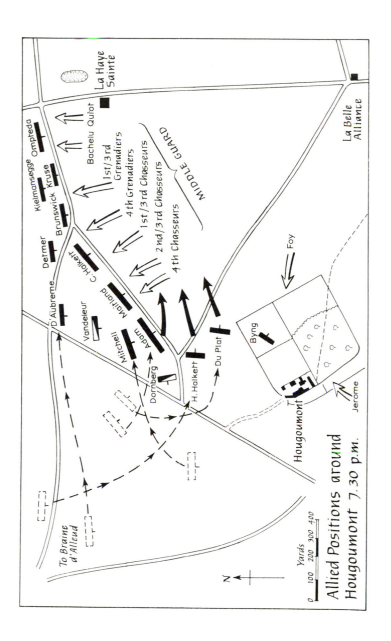

La Haye Sainte

Ompteda
Kielmansegge
Brunswick Kruse
Detmer
D'Aubreme
C. Halkett
Vandeleur
Mitchell
Maitland
Dornberg
Adam
H. Halkett
Du Plat
Byng
Hougoumont
Jerome

Bachelu Quiot

1st/3rd Grenadiers
4th Grenadiers
1st/3rd Chasseurs
2nd/3rd Chasseurs
4th Chasseurs

MIDDLE GUARD

Foy

La Belle Alliance

To Braine d'Alleud

Yards
0   100 200 300 400

N

Allied Positions around
Hougoumont 7.30 p.m.

in a space of a few minutes every officer ... became a casualty and command passed to the senior Sergeant.'

Some of the French cavalry had, during this encounter, managed to penetrate behind Hougoumont and attack the ridge to the north. This was a dangerous threat, but was countered by Adam's Brigade, which Wellington had moved forward earlier to a position on the right of Maitland's Brigade. Unfortunately Colonel du Plat, commanding the K.G.L. Brigade, was killed at about this time.

Seventh French Attack[2]

The Third Guards had suffered heavy casualties in this action, but there was yet another to be survived. At about 1830 the gallant K.G.L., under Major Baring, had finally been driven out of La Haye Sainte when their ammunition ran out. This meant that the French had troops to spare, and they launched a final assault on Hougoumont. The remnants of Foy's Division advanced yet again against the south and east sides of the orchard, while Jerome launched yet another assault on the farm.

'We were again outflanked,' recalled Hepburn, 'and driven back to our friendly Hollow Way, and again the fire of the Coldstream did us good service. In fact, it was this fire that constituted the strength of the post. We once more advanced and resumed our station along the front edge, from whence there was no further effort to dislodge us.'

He went on to add: 'During this time I knew nothing of what was passing elsewhere.'

'La Garde Recule'
In fact a great deal was going on elsewhere. At 7.30pm Napoleon at last committed his invincible Imperial Guard. Two columns, totalling at least 3,000 veterans of the Middle Guard, led by Marshal Ney himself, were launched by Napoleon in a final,

[2] See map on page 11.

desperate bid to break the Allied line. Two battalions of Grenadiers[3] advanced against Colonel C. Halkett's Brigade, while three battalions of Chasseurs[4] attacked Maitland's Guards Brigade. Two battalions were held back in reserve.

But Wellington, always so brilliant at anticipating his opponents' moves, had already strengthened his centre, and had also positioned himself between Adam's and Maitland's Brigades, where his instinct told him that the final enemy onslaught was most likely to fall.

Maitland's 1st Guards Brigade had by now been reduced to about 1,500 men, including Lord Saltoun's light companies, who had already endured so much fierce fighting in the orchard at Hougoumont. The men had been ordered to lie down just behind the crest of the ridge,[5] so as to escape the hail of artillery and musket fire that was sweeping the ridge. They could not, therefore, see the French advancing upon them, but they could hear the shouts of '*En avant. Vive l'Empereur*' coming ever closer.

Wellington, however, on horseback just beside them, could see the five columns of the Middle Guard steadily advancing up the slope towards him, while across the valley Napoleon stared through the smoke, watching them fade into the gathering gloom.

Wellington waited calmly until the enemy were only some forty paces distant, and then called out to the Brigade Commander.

'Now, Maitland. Now's your time.'

And a few seconds later:

'Stand up, Guards. Make ready. Fire.'

As the Guards rose to their feet, the two sides saw each other for the first time. The first deadly volley from the British struck the packed ranks of the Imperial Guard and 300 of them fell. Bolton's and Napier's Batteries joined in with a barrage of

[3] 1st/3rd and 4th Battalions.
[4] 1st/3rd, 2nd/3rd and 4th Battalions.
[5] They were either side of and just behind the stone by the road that today marks the monument to Captain Mercer.

grapeshot, which did terrible damage.

Shoulder to shoulder in column, the French could neither return the fire nor deploy. For ten long minutes they tried to advance, but could not move. The devastating volleys continued to thud into their helpless ranks. It was a desperate, bloody struggle of wills between the two bodies of élite troops.

Then, suddenly, it was the Imperial Guard who wavered.

'Now's the time, my boys,' called Lord Saltoun, still in the thick of the fighting, and the First Guards charged with fixed bayonets.

At the same time Colonel Colborne, commanding the 52nd (Oxfordshire Light Infantry) from Adam's 3rd Brigade[6] on the right of the Guards, manoeuvred his men so that they could enfilade the entire enemy column. After one deadly volley they charged, together with the Guards and the 71st and 95th from Adam's Brigade.

For many long minutes, the French faced them in a fierce fire fight, but finally it was they who turned and showed their backs. Unbelieving, both British and French watched the impossible happen. The Imperial Guard were in retreat; they had been beaten. The Emperor's invincible Grenadiers had failed him.

'*La Garde recule.*'

Those three words, spelt, in effect, the defeat of France. Napoleon had gambled all and had lost.

---

[6] Adam's, Du Plat's and H. Halkett's Brigades were at this stage all positioned just to the north-east of the orchard in Hougoumont which thus formed a base for their attack against the flank of the Imperial Guard.

Chapter 11
'You See, the Guards Held Hougoumont'

'The Line Will Advance,'

Round Hougoumont the bitter fighting continued unabated, with neither side being aware of the fate of the Imperial Guard. But Wellington, on the ridge behind them, could see that almost everywhere except at Hougoumont the enemy were now in full retreat. For a moment he watched, then lifted his hat and waved it in the direction of the fleeing French.

'The line will advance.'

Some of his staff ventured to suggest that this was rather rash.

'Oh, damn it,' came the retort. 'In for a penny, in for a pound.'

Colonel Hepburn, in the orchard, was the first to hear the great news, for he was nearest to the Duke. 'A staff officer came up from the left at full gallop,' he recorded, 'with orders for an immediate advance, stating that the whole army was moving on to the Charge. We passed the hedge and moved upon the troops in the cornfield, who retired in no order and almost without firing.'

With a hoarse cheer from parched throats, the Third Guards joined in the pursuit, as the whole Allied line, now barely 40,000 strong, swept forward. But Hepburn's men were too exhausted to pursue the enemy very far, and they were content to leave that to the comparatively fresh, vengeful Prussians, who hunted them down with relish.

As the Allied line moved forward, the troops in Hougoumont remained at their posts. Wearily they watched in the gathering gloom as the enemy, who for the last nine hours had done their best to kill them, now disappeared into the wood, where at dawn that same day (a lifetime ago, it seemed) it had all started. Private Clay was one of the survivors in Hougoumont.

'We kept a watchful eye on the enemy,' he recorded, 'whose attacks now became less frequent...

'The firing shortly ceased and our complete victory was announced in our little garrison. We had a look around and saw the sad havoc the enemy had made of our fortress. The fire, unobstructed, continued its ravages and, having been unnoticed by us in eagerness of the conflict, destroyed many of the buildings where in the early part of the action many of the helpless wounded of both armies had been posted for security.

'I went into a kind of kitchen and found the wounded being arranged all around as far as possible out of harm's way; there was a great admixture of different countries. About this time some Belgian soldiers with others who were looking out for their wounded or missing comrades saw some Frenchmen among the wounded and began to menace the poor fellows with their bayonets and would have acted violently towards them had we not interfered in [sic] their behalf.

'On again going into the yard, it being evening, and seeing a clear glowing fire rising from the ruins of a stable or some other outhouse, I took the opportunity of cooking the remaining portion of pork which I had stored away in my haversack. I placed it upon the fire and quietly awaited its being cooked, but discovered that the glow of the fire arose from the half-consumed body of some party who had fallen in the contest. My meat, which was unsavoury in the morning, became much more so by its redressing, and having now found a little meal in a cooking pot hanging over a small fire which was smothered with dust and fragments from the broken ruins but sufficiently cooked, I most gladly partook of it. I have no recollections of our having any other refreshment either on that or the previous day, with the exception of our ration of liquor . . . and a small amount of bread which we found at Quatre Bras amongst the slain.'

After a while the Coldstreamers in Hougoumont were ordered to move back and bivouack for the night in a field just behind the farm, where they joined their 7 and 8 Companies. The Third Guards too returned from the pursuit and bivouacked nearby, joining up with their light company who had been with the Coldstream in Hougoumont all day.

The Cost

At the Roll Call that evening there were many names that went unanswered in both battalions. The losses were not as grim as in some of the regiments on the main position, but they were heavy enough.

The Coldstream Guards lost 348 all ranks, while the Third Guards casualties were 236. The light companies of the First Guards lost two thirds of their strength during their time in the orchard.

Altogether the Allied troops involved in the defence of Hougoumont suffered some 1,500 casualties,[1] against 5,000 French killed and wounded.

Among the wounded should be remembered Mrs Osborne, the wife of Private George Osborne of the Third Guards, whom she had married at Enghein on St George's Day (23 April) that year. She was in the thick of the fighting all day, looking after the wounded, and tearing up her own spare clothing to make bandages. She was eventually severely wounded herself by a musket shot in the arm and left breast, but she survived. As a result of recommendations by Lieutenant-Colonel Edward Bowater, whose wound she had dressed on the battlefield, she was later awarded the Queen's Bounty.

[1] This includes the Nassauers, Hanoverians and Brunswick units, as well as 2nd Guards Brigade, Du Plat's Brigade and H. Halkett's Hanoverian Brigade. British casualty figures are taken from the official Casualty Returns of 13 April 1816.

Relative Strengths

There are varying accounts of the numbers involved on each side in the struggle for Hougoumont. There is little doubt that the French committed 13–15,000 troops to their continuous attacks on the farm and orchard. This represented the major part of three divisions (Jerome, Foy and Bachelu) which might otherwise have been available for other attacks.

Altogether, Wellington committed a maximum of 3,500 troops to the actual defence of Hougoumont, with perhaps a further 2,500 in support behind the farm.

The figures of 2,000 British men against 13,000 French are often quoted, but they usually refer to the 1,800 men of the Guards involved, which ignores the Nassauers and Hanoverians as well as the two K.G.L. battalions who were used to support the Third Guards in the orchard during the afternoon.

Even on the basis of around 6,000 Allied troops defending Hougoumont against some 14,000 Frenchmen attacking it, this was a most satisfactory and economical ratio from Wellington's point of view. He fed in reinforcements only as essential, and yet effectively tied down most of Reille's Corps for the entire day. Nor did he weaken his centre, as Napoleon had hoped he would.

Wellington's Despatch

That night Wellington wrote in his Despatch:

> 'It gives me the greatest satisfaction to assure your Lordship that the army never upon any occasion conducted itself better. The Division of Guards ... set an example which was followed by all.'

And of the defence of Hougoumont, he reported:

> 'At about ten o'clock [sic] he [Napoleon] commenced a furious attack upon our post at Hougoumont. I had occu-

pied that post with a detachment from General Byng's Brigade of Guards, which was in position to its rear, and it was for some time under the command of Lieutenant-Colonel Macdonald [sic] and afterwards of Colonel Home;[2] and I am happy to add that it was maintained throughout the day with the utmost gallantry by these brave troops, notwithstanding the repeated efforts of large bodies of the enemy to obtain possession of it.'

Creevey related that as the Duke was at work on his Despatch, he 'praised greatly those Guards who kept the farm against the repeated attacks of the French', and also commented, 'You may depend upon it that no troops but the British could have held Hougoumont and only the best of them at that.'

After it was all over the Duke remembered that General Müffling had, on the evening before the battle, ventured to question whether Hougoumont was defensible at all, and he could not resist making his point, with the brief comment: 'You see, the Guards held Hougoumont.'

[2] This should have read Colonel Hepburn.

Chapter 12
After the Battle

The Morning After

Hougoumont presented a grim picture indeed the next morning. Most of the buildings were gutted ruins, some still smouldering. Bodies of French, British and German soldiers lay everywhere; some were still in their muddy, bloodstained uniforms, but most of them had already been stripped bare overnight by pillagers, who continued their soulless robbery throughout the day.

One of the saddest tasks was to dig a huge pit on the south side of the farm, into which were tipped the bodies with little or no ceremony, or they were burned, as was the custom in those days, before there were military cemeteries.

The walls of the few buildings still standing were heavily pockmarked with bullet holes and battered by shells. The trees were equally pitted, broken and stripped of their foliage. The gardener was wandering round the scene of devastation, aghast at the damage, and wondering what would happen now.

The next day Private Clay 'received orders' to accompany a Corporal to the burning ruins of Hougoumont, and by the haystack he found the bodies of several of his comrades in arms. 'Apparently they were entire,' he wrote, 'but on touching them I found them completely dried up by the heat.'

He then set off with the rest of his Regiment to march back to Nivelles, where,

> 'having arrived at a small grass field in sight of Nivelles, we halted for the night. . . . There was a buzz of congratulating

6 Burying the Dead at Hougoumont. A painting by D.
Dighton. By courtesy of Windsor Castle Royal Library.
© 1991. Her Majesty The Queen.

interchanges taking place with men of different companies,
their townsmen and old acquaintances ... each listening to
the narrative of his comrade, having been separated from
each other during the contest. Had any of our enquiring
friends in England been present in this sad field in which
was our bivouac, they would have listened with the deepest
interest to the tales that were told on the night of 19th June,
1815.'

Three Englishmen who visited Hougoumont in July, 1815, only
weeks after the battle, described the scene:[1]

'Every tree in the wood at Hougoumont is pierced with
balls; in one alone I counted the holes where upwards of
thirty had lodged ... huge piles of human ashes, dreadfully

[1] *Account of a Visit to Waterloo.*

offensive in smell, are all that now remain of the heroes who
fought and fell upon this fatal spot. . . . The poor country-
man who, with his wife[2] and family, occupied the gardener's
house still inhabit a miserable shed among the deserted
ruins, and pointed out with superstitious reverence the
little chapel belonging to the château which stood alone
uninjured in the midst of the blackened walls and fallen
beams . . . a more mournful scene than this ruined château
and wood cannot possibly be imagined.'

Another visitor to the battlefield was John Scott who described
what he found there in 1815:[3]

'The buildings of Hougoumont were infinitely more shat-
tered than even those at La Haye Sainte. . . . In one single
spot fifty dead bodies lay close together where they fell.
Near this there was a black scorched place where 600 human
corpses, found in the grounds, were collected and burned.
Fire had been set to the buildings . . . and the whole place
seemed to have been the theatre of a supernatural mischief –
some celebration of infernal rites.'

'*The Bravest Man in England*'
All ranks who took part in the Battle of Waterloo received in
1816 a silver Waterloo Medal, the first general issue made to the
British Army. In addition, they had the letters 'W.M.' (Waterloo
Man) put in red after their names in the records; of greater
importance, perhaps, was that this counted as two years' extra
service.
    Officers in the Household Cavalry and Foot Guards benefited
too, in that the privilege of 'double rank'[4] was extended to

---

[2] This is the only known reference to the gardener's wife, who was not at
Hougoumont during the battle.
[3] *Paris Revisited by way of Brussels (including a walk over the field of battle of
Waterloo)*. John Scott, 1816.
[4] See page 28. (Note 6)

include Ensigns, who were now also given the rank of Lieutenant.

Corporal James Graham of the Coldstream Guards (now a
Sergeant) and Sergeant Fraser of the Third Guards were both
awarded a special medal for their gallantry at Hougoumont.
Sergeant Graham was also nominated by Wellington for an
annuity of £10 a year, which had been offered by a patriotic
citizen, the Reverend John Norcross, Rector of Framlingham in
Suffolk, to be given to 'one of his brave countrymen, who fought
in the late tremendous but glorious conflict'.

Unfortunately, after only two years, the Rector went bankrupt
and the annuity ceased. But when he died some time later, he
left £500 to be given to 'the bravest man in England'. Wellington
was asked to nominate this individual, and he wrote: 'The
success of the Battle of Waterloo turned on the closing of the
gates at Hougoumont. The gates were closed in the most cour-
ageous manner at [sic] the very nick of time by the efforts of Sir
J. Macdonell.[5] I cannot help thinking Sir James is the man to
whom you should give the £500.'

So it was settled, but the gallant Colonel immediately shared
his award with Sergeant Graham, declaring, 'I cannot claim all
the merit due to the closing of the gates of Hougoumont, for
Sergeant John [sic][6] Graham, who saw the importance of the
step, rushed forward and together we shut the gates.'

Château de Hougoumont

The Château de Hougoumont was clearly uninhabitable after
the battle, and the property was put on the market later that
year by the owner, Chevalier de Louville. It was bought on 7
May, 1816, by Count Francois-Xavier de Robiano for 40,000
francs. It has remained in his family ever since, and is owned
today, through inheritance, by the Comtesse d'Oultrement.

The farm continued to be occupied and run by a tenant, and

[5] He had been knighted after Waterloo.

[6] This must be an error by Colonel Macdonell. It should be 'James'.

7 The South Gate at Hougoumont in 1817. A drawing by
Richenda Gurney.

most of the farm buildings were restored to a usable state, though
those on the north and east sides were not rebuilt.

The remains of the château gradually disappeared, much of
the stone being used to build a *Café des Ruines* at the junction
of the drive from Hougoumont with the Nivelles road.[7] Parts of
the château were also incorporated into the new farm, and by
about 1860 it was all gone; today only the foundations of the
walls remain, although the chapel next to it is still standing, very
little changed.

In the years after Waterloo Hougoumont was visited by many
travellers and sightseers, mostly from Britain, and it is possible
to learn from their descriptions and drawings what changes took
place. Some of these visitors, including Byron and Shelley,
inscribed their names on the wall of the chapel, but in 1848 the

---

[7] The café subsequently became a farmhouse, and remained so until the motorway was built in the 1970s.

74

8 The ruins of the Chateau de Hougoumont in 1817. A
drawing by Richenda Gurney.

walls were painted over, and these *graffiti* removed.

The battlefield changed little over the next 100 years, but in
March, 1914, came a threat to build a new road across the middle
of it. Thanks to the determined efforts of the 5th Duke of
Wellington, supported by le Comte Snoy, who owned much of
the land, and by others, the proposal was defeated and the
historic site was saved. An Act of the Belgian Parliament dated
26 March, 1914, declared the whole battlefield to be a Protected
Area, which it happily remains today.

Nevertheless a further attempt was made in the 1960s to
construct a motorway across it, but this was fortunately
prevented. This time it was the 8th Duke of Wellington who
intervened, supported by the British Ambassador and many
others, and the highway was diverted to run just north of the
ridge of Mont St Jean; it still however runs through the position
of Byng's Brigade north of Hougoumont.

One major change from 1815 is Lion Hill, which was raised

in the 1820s as a monument to the Prince of Orange. This dominant artificial landmark not only altered the skyline, but also meant that the level of the ground all round it as far as the Brussels road was lowered by at least three feet, because of the soil that was removed to build the mound.

Apart from Lion Hill, the battlefield is largely unchanged and it is not difficult to work out the dispositions of both sides, and to follow the events of that dramatic day. It is possible to stand exactly where Wellington and Napoleon must have stood, and to survey the scene much as they did. Most people are struck by how small the actual battlefield is, a mere two miles by one mile approximately, so that the two commanders could see each other across the valley.

It is a unique historic heritage, and it is indeed to be hoped that it will now forever be preserved as such.

Chapter 13
A Tour of Hougoumont Today

Hougoumont today is an integral part of the battlefield, but it is also a private, tenanted farm, occupied and run by Monsieur Roger Temmerman and his family. His life is farming, but he is well aware of the great historic significance of his home and he looks on it as his duty to accept the constant stream of visitors.

The whole area of Hougoumont is open to the public, with the proviso that there is no access to the interior of any buildings, and sightseeing must not interfere with farming activities. One result of this is that visitors' vehicles are *not* allowed right up to the farm, but must be left in the small car park 150 yards short of the North Gate. Hougoumont is in any case a spot that should be visited on foot, if one is to appreciate fully the events of 18 June, 1815.

The Approach Road
The farm road from the car park to the North Gate was originally the *drive* to the château and was lined by elms, which are no longer standing.

To the left is a *wood* that was not there in 1815, and the slope on which it now stands was the forward part of the ridge held by Byng's Brigade at the start of the battle. To the right of the drive can be seen the low *ridge* on which the French placed some guns.

The North Gate
As one approaches Hougoumont, the **Great Barn** forms the west side of the farm gate, while straight ahead is the **North Gate**.

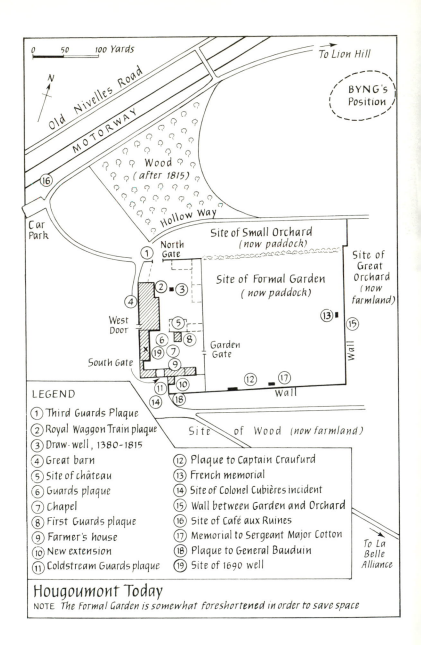

0 50 100 Yards

N

To Lion Hill

BYNG's Position

Old Nivelles Road

MOTORWAY

(16)

Car Park

Wood (after 1815)

Hollow Way

North Gate

Site of Small Orchard (now paddock)

Site of Great Orchard (now farmland)

Site of Formal Garden (now paddock)

(1)

(2) ■ (3)

(4)

West Door

(5)

(6) (8)

(19) (7)

× (9)

South Gate

(11) (10)

(14) (18)

Garden Gate

(13) ■ (15)

Wall

(12) ■ (17)

Wall

Site of Wood (now farmland)

LEGEND

(1) Third Guards Plaque
(2) Royal Waggon Train plaque
(3) Draw-well, 1380-1815
(4) Great barn
(5) Site of château
(6) Guards plaque
(7) Chapel
(8) First Guards plaque
(9) Farmer's house
(10) New extension
(11) Coldstream Guards plaque

(12) Plaque to Captain Craufurd
(13) French memorial
(14) Site of Colonel Cubières incident
(15) Wall between Garden and Orchard
(16) Site of Café aux Ruines
(17) Memorial to Sergeant Major Cotton
(18) Plaque to General Bauduin
(19) Site of 1690 well

To La Belle Alliance

Hougoumont Today

NOTE The Formal Garden is somewhat foreshortened in order to save space

78

9 Hougoumont from the North, showing the Great Barn and North Gate.

This is the famous gate that was closed 'at the very nick of time', and in 1815 it was the main entrance to Hougoumont. Then it was a solid, wooden gate with two panels and a timber cross-beam above (see page 44). This has now gone, and there is just a small, ironwork gate, through which it is possible to see the farmyard, the draw-well, the chapel, and in the distance, the gardener's house (now occupied by the farmer).

The outbuildings that stood on either side of the gate in 1815 have disappeared, but the high wall remains.

On the wall to the right or west of the gate is a *plaque to the officers and men of the 2nd Battalion Third Guards*, (now the Scots Guards), who died defending the farm. It includes a star which is a copy of the medal that was specially struck for Sergeant Fraser and awarded to him for his outstanding bravery.

This plaque was unveiled on 12 July, 1958, with a Guard of Honour from Left Flank, 2nd Battalion Scots Guards, which

is the company descended from the 'Light Company' of the
Regiment that fought at Hougoumont. Among those present
was the grandson of Private Matthew Clay of the Third Guards;
he wore his grandfather's Waterloo Medal for the occasion.

The plaque was refurbished in 1990.

The Farmyard

Remembering the bitter struggle round the North Gate, it does
not somehow seem right to be able to stroll through today,
unopposed, and, once inside, to stand in the **Farmyard**, where
those Frenchmen who did force their way in through the gate
all fell in desperate hand-to-hand combat. The image of that
scene is still very vivid.

On the wall of the Great Barn just inside the North Gate is a
plaque to the Royal Waggon Train, erected in 1979, and it must
have been just about there that Private Brewer thankfully halted
his tumbril of vital ammunition after running the gauntlet

10 The view through the North Gate, showing the draw-
   well, Chapel and Gardener's House in the background,
   and the Scots Guards plaque on the wall.

11 The Farmyard with the Draw-Well in the foreground and the Chapel and Gardener's House behind.

outside and reaching the comparative safety of the buildings.

Just to the left of the path in the farmyard is the **Draw Well** that was 'lost' after the battle until it was rediscovered and excavated by Derek Saunders in 1985. It was mentioned by Victor Hugo in his epic *Les Miserables*, where he described how '300 bodies were thrown down the well ... the faint cries of those not yet dead haunting the memory'. But when the well was excavated 170 years later no human remains were found, nor even any relics of the battle – just a few animal bones.[1]

Nothing remains of the château today, though Derek Saunders and his team have uncovered most of the foundations, so that it is possible to see the outline of where it stood.

[1] The base has been rebuilt by Derek Saunders, and it is hoped one day when funds are available, to restore the well-head to what it was in 1815.

ROYAL WAGGON TRAIN

ROYAL WAGGON TRAIN

IN MEMORY OF
THE OFFICERS AND MEN
OF THE ROYAL WAGGON TRAIN
WHO TOOK PART IN THE
DEFENCE OF HOUGOUMONT
18TH JUNE 1815

THIS TABLET WAS ERECTED IN 1979
BY THE ROYAL CORPS OF TRANSPORT
THE SUCCESSORS OF
THE ROYAL WAGGON TRAIN

12 The Plaque to the Royal Waggon Train.

The Chapel

The **chapel** still stands, little changed since the battle, and it is one of the most moving spots in Hougoumont. Somehow it survived the fire that destroyed the château alongside it. One can still see the figure of Christ Crucified, with the feet charred and blackened by the flames that licked under the door of the chapel during the battle.

Much work was done on the chapel in 1965 to mark the 150th

anniversary of the Battle. The interior was re-decorated by men of the Coldstream Guards, while the pioneers of the Scots Guards carved the wooden cross that stands on the altar.[2] It was consecrated in the Guards Chapel in London on Sunday, 13 June, 1965, and was then placed in Hougoumont Chapel on 18 June by a detachment from 2nd Battalion, Scots Guards.

On the West wall of the Chapel is a large *bronze plaque* requesting due respect for this sacred building round which so many died. It is written in three languages (English, French and German), and the inscription reads:

> 'To the Memory of the Brave Dead this tablet was erected by His Britannic Majesty's Brigade of Guards and by Comte Charles van der Burch. 1907.'[3]

This tribute was erected at the instigation of Lieutenant-Colonel McCartney-Filgate of the Royal Irish Rifles, who visited Hougoumont in 1905 and was dismayed to find how dilapidated the whole place was. The tablet was installed at his own expense, and was unveiled by the British Ambassador on 11 April, 1907.

A *stone plaque* was also erected in 1977 on the east wall of the chapel to the memory of those of the First Guards who died at Hougoumont, defending the orchard.

The Formal Garden

Between the château and the garden once stood the **Farmer's House**, but nothing now remains except the outline of the walls, excavated and raised by Derek Saunders. Continuing on towards the garden one comes to a metal farm gate, which is roughly where the arched opening and **Garden Gate** were in 1815. Just

---

[2] The badges of the three Guards Regiments who held Hougoumont are carved on the base of the cross, and are in the order of the positions they held there. i.e. Grenadier Guards on the left, Coldstream Guards in the centre and Scots Guards on the right.

[3] The owner of Hougoumont at the time who had succeeded his father-in-law, le Comte de Robiano, in the 1890's.

AUX
SOLDATS
FRANÇAIS
MORTS
A
HOUGOUMONT
18 JUIN 1815

13 The French Memorial in the Formal Garden.

84

14 The view looking north-east from the Garden towards
the Lion Hill, with the ridge held by 1st Guards Brigade
on the left.

the other side of the wall was a paved and balustraded terrace,
where the owners of the château and their guests used to sit and
admire the beautiful **Formal Garden**. Now it is all put down
to grass for grazing.

On the north side of the garden a few trees remain which mark
the edge of the **Small Orchard**, which in 1815 was bordered
by a hedge rather than a wall. Beyond the small orchard is the
Hollow Way.

Along the south side of the garden runs a long red-brick *wall*,
with white-lined loopholes still in it; some were always there
and others, that were made just for the battle, have since been
bricked up.

In this south wall there are two *Plaques* to officers who died
in the fighting there. One is to Captain John Lucie Blackman of
the Coldstream Guards, the other to Captain Thomas Craufurd
of the Third Guards.[4]

Towards the middle of the garden is the *tombstone of Private
(later Sergeant-Major) Edward Cotton* of the 7th Hussars. He
fought at Waterloo and returned some 20 years later; having
married a local girl, he settled down as a 'Guide and Describer

[4] Originally buried in the garden, their remains were moved in 1890 to the
Waterloo Crypt in the Cemetery at Evre.

85

of the Battle' until his death in 1849. He also wrote a book entitled *A Voice from Waterloo*, which is of considerable value because he showed round the battlefield many officers who had fought there, and so was able to obtain their first-hand accounts of events.

Towards the east end of the Garden is an impressive granite *Monument to the French soldiers* who died attacking Hougoumont (although none of them actually succeeded in reaching the garden). It was erected in 1913 on the initiative of the Belgian historian, Hector Fleischmann, author of *La tragique histoire du château d'Hougoumont*. The inscription is said to have been dictated by Napoleon himself, while in exile on St Helena, and it reads:

'La terre paraissait orgueilleuse de porter tant de braves.'[5]

The Great Orchard

At the end of the meadow that was once the Formal Garden, and beyond the Monument to the French, is a wall, which in 1815 ran between the garden and the **Great Orchard**.[6] This was the line of defence that was manned by the Coldstream Guards, and proved so effective because from behind it they were able to pour a devastating fire into the flank of every French attack across the Great Orchard.

The ground that was the Great Orchard is now agricultural land and there are no trees on it.[7] To the right is the valley from which came all the French attacks, while straight ahead can be seen Lion Hill; to the left is the continuation of the Hollow Way, and beyond it the ridge on which Byng's Second Guards Brigade was positioned. Throughout the battle the French never ceased to attack the Great Orchard, but it was tenaciously defended by

---

[5] 'The ground seemed proud to hold so many fine men.' The monument was restored in 1954 by the *Sociéte Belge d'Études Napoleoniennes*.

[6] The eastern end of the Formal Garden (where the Monument to the French stands) is often mistaken for the Great Orchard, even by some of the local guides.

[7] When Monsieur Temmerman's father, Frans, took over the farm in 1947, a few trees remained, but they were later removed.

15 The South Gate from the area of the Haystack – which is today still located in the area where it was in 1815.

the First and then the Third Guards, and changed hands many times.

The Great Orchard extended for some 300 yards, and between it and Lion Hill is the long slope up which charged the French cavalry. One can imagine how the Third Guards watched the awesome sight, and opened fire at the horsemen as they thundered past. The Imperial Guard also tramped up the same slope till they came up against Maitland's 1st Guards Brigade on the ridge to the left.

The Hollow Way
Below the ridge the **Hollow Way** continues in the low ground, and one can see why it played such a significant part as a supply route between Hougoumont and the main position. It was bordered on the orchard side by a substantial hedge and ditch, and it was probably into this that Matthew Clay fell and had difficulty in extricating himself.[8]

The Gardener's House
Returning to the Garden Gate, one sees the **Gardener's House**

[8] See Page 27.

on one's left. Despite being in the thick of the fighting all day, it was not destroyed or even burned, though it has quite a few bullet holes still visible in it today. A change since 1815 is that a new dining-room extension has been built onto the south side in what was the small garden.

The South Gate

The **South Gate** and the archway are virtually unchanged from 1815, and it is easy to see how the accurate musket fire from the windows and walls made it impossible for the French to penetrate that side of Hougoumont at all.

The defence of this sector was the task of 2nd Battalion Coldstream Guards and a *Plaque* to commemorate them was placed on the wall by the gate in 1965.

The Wood

The scene immediately to the south of Hougoumont is very different today from what it was in 1815, chiefly because **the Wood** has disappeared. The trees were all badly damaged in the

16 The view looking south from the South Gate towards where the Wood was, with three dead trees which must have stood on its North edge.

17 The South Wall of the Garden running east from the Gardener's House, with loopholes still visible.

battle and many were cut down to provide firewood for the burning of the bodies in the area. Just three aged and ailing elms still stand, marking what was the north edge of the wood.

The open space still existing between the former edge of the wood and the wall of the farm is the 30-yard gap that the attackers found so impossible to cross, and the French have recently placed a *plaque* in the wall here in memory of General Bauduin who died in the first attack on Hougoumont.

A *track* still runs half-left from Hougoumont towards La Belle Alliance and if one walks along it for a hundred yards there is a good view of Hougoumont from the enemy point of view and of the loopholed garden wall.

Where the wood once stood the ground falls away to the valley where Reille's corps was formed up, with arms piled, awaiting the order to advance against Hougoumont, which they could not see until they got to within some 200 yards of it.

The Lane

Moving right from the South Gate one can walk round the outside of the farm along the lane where Matthew Clay and his comrade, Private Gann, found themselves cut off and under heavy fire, before escaping back through the North Gate.

It was near here that Colonel Cubières of the Light Regiment was unhorsed by Sergeant Fraser of the Third Guards, and where Colonel Woodford and his Coldstream Guards successfully drove the French back from the North Gate. In the wall of the Great Barn on the right can be seen the outline of the small West Door.

Finis

So, we end up once more at the famous gates of Hougoumont upon the closing of which 'rested the outcome of the Battle of Waterloo'.

APPENDIX A

Sequence of events at Hougoumont

17th June 1815

Serial	*Approximate Time*	*Event at Hougoumont*	*Commander*	*Main Battle*
1	1700	1st and 2nd Guards Brigades arrive at Mont St Jean	Cooke	
2	1900	Light Companies, 1st Guards Brigade occupy Orchard	Saltoun	
3	1900	Light Companies, 2nd Guards Brigade occupy farm	Macdonell	
4	Evening	French cavalry patrol driven off	Macdonell	
5	Evening	Picquet from Third Guards posted in Wood	Evelyn	

18th June 1815

6	Dawn	Saltoun in Orchard relieved by Nassauers and Hanoverians	Saltoun	
7	Early morning	Wellington visits Saltoun	Wellington	
8	Early morning	Wellington orders Nassauers and Hanoverians to move forward		

91

Serial	Approximate Time	Event at Hougoumont	Commander	Main Battle
		and occupy Wood		
9	Early Morning	Wellington orders Third Guards to move from Garden to Lane	Evelyn	0900. Napoleon holds conference
10	About 1100	Light Companies, First Guards rejoin 1st Guards Brigade		1000. Napoleon reviews troops
11	1130	*First French attack* – against Wood from South	Bauduin	
12	1150	Nassauers and Hanoverians driven out of Wood and back into Orchard		
13	1150	Saltoun and light companies advance and recapture Orchard	Saltoun	
14	1200	*Second French Attack* – against West side of Hougoumont	Soye	
15	1230	Closing of the Gates	Macdonell	
16	1300	Counter-attack by 2nd Battalion Coldstream Guards, who	Woodford	

Serial	Approximate Time	Event at Hougoumont	Commander	Main Battle
		then move into Farm		
17	1300 (or probably later)	Ammunition tumbril arrives		
18	1245	*Third French Attack* – against Orchard	Gautier	1300. Prussians in sight
19	1330	Counter-attack against Orchard by two companies of Third Guards	Home	1300. French bombardment starts
20		French bring up howitzer and shell Hougoumont from Wood		1345. French attack by d'Erlon's Corps
21		Saltoun unsuccessfully attacks howitzer in Wood	Saltoun	
22	1400	*Fourth French Attack.* Against Orchard from East. Saltoun and light companies driven back	Foy	
23	1400	Three companies of Third Guards relieve Saltoun in Orchard	Hepburn	
24	1400	Wellington moves H. Halkett's		

Serial	Approximate Time	Event at Hougoumont	Commander	Main Battle
		Brigade forward to replace 2nd Guards Brigade, and reinforces troops in Orchard		
25		Third Guards regain Orchard	Hepburn	
26	Between 1400 and 1500	*Fifth French Attack.* Against Orchard from South East. Stopped by artillery fire	Bachelu Foy	1430. Allied cavalry charge French infantry
27	1500	Hougoumont set on fire		
28	1600	*Sixth French Attack* Against Orchard from the South East	Bachelu Foy	1600. First French cavalry charge
29		Counter-attack by Third Guards regains Orchard	Hepburn	1630. Prussians start to debouch
30	1600 or earlier	Hepburn takes over command of 2nd Guards Brigade	Hepburn	1700. Prussians capture Plancenoit
31		Home takes over command of Third Guards	Home	
32	1730			Second French Cavalry charge
33	1830	*Seventh French*	Foy	1830.

Serial	Approximate Time	Event at Hougoumont	Commander	Main Battle
		Attack. Against Orchard from South East		French capture La Haye Sainte
34		Counter-attack by Third Guards,	Home	1830. Prussians close in on French right
35				1930. Attack by French Imperial Guard
36	2015	General Allied advance		2000. Imperial Guard repulsed
37				2115. Wellington and Blücher meet.

APPENDIX B

Personalities at Hougoumont

BAIRD, Ensign David. Third Guards
Joined Third Guards in 1812. Served in 7 Company at Waterloo.
Severely wounded. Retired before 1824. Succeeded to Baronetcy in
1829. Died 1851.

BREWER, Private Joseph. Waggon Train
A mystery figure, variously described as Private and Corporal; Joseph
and Gregory; Brewer and Brewster. Said to have transferred from the
Waggon Train to the Third Guards after Waterloo, but does not appear
in the records of the Third Guards.

BYNG, Major-General Sir John. Third Guards
Joined Third Guards in 1804. Twice received the thanks of Parliament
for distinguished service, once in the Peninsular War and again after
Waterloo. Commanded 2nd Guards Brigade at Waterloo and took over
command of 1st Division when Cooke was wounded. Became a Field-
Marshal in 1855. Appointed G.C.B., G.C.H., K.M.T., K.St G., P.C.[1]
Created Baron Strafford in 1835 and Earl of Strafford in 1847. Became
Colonel, Coldstream Guards in 1850. Died 1860.

CLAY, Private Matthew. Third Guards
Enlisted into the Third Guards from the Nottinghamshire Militia in
1813. Aged 20 in 1815. Became a Drill Sergeant in Third Guards in
1828 and retired in 1833. Became Sergeant-Major of the Bedfordshire
Militia.

COOKE, Major-General George. First Guards
Joined First Guards in 1784. Wounded in Holland 1799. Fought in
Peninsular War. Major-General 1811. Commanded 1st Division at
Waterloo. Severely wounded and lost an arm. K.C.B. K.St G. Colonel-
in-Chief 40th Foot. Died 1837.

DASHWOOD, Lt-Colonel Charles. Third Guards
Joined Third Guards in 1803. Served in Peninsular War. Won Gold

---

[1] G.C.H.   Knight Grand Cross of Hanover.
  K.M.T.   Knight of Maria Theresa of Austria.
  K.St G.   Knight of St George of Russia.

Medal at Nive. 1813. Commanded the Light Company at Waterloo. Retired 1823. Died 1832.

EVELYN, Captain George. Third Guards
Joined Third Guards in 1810. Served in Light Company at Waterloo. Retired 1821. Died 1829.

DRUMMOND, Ensign Berkeley. Third Guards
Joined Third Guards in 1812. Acting Adjutant at Waterloo. Was responsible for delivery of tumbril of ammunition to Hougoumont. Attained rank of General. Retired 1850. Appointed Groom in Waiting to the Queen. Died 1860.

FRASER, Sergeant Ralph. Third Guards
Served in Egypt, Hanover, Copenhagen and Peninsular War. Twice severely wounded. Fought at Hougoumont, and unhorsed Colonel Cubières. Helped to close the gates. Received a special medal for his gallantry. Discharged in 1818 'in consequence of long service and being worn out.' Became a Bedesman at Westminster Abbey, and lived till aged 80, dying in 1862.

GOOCH, Ensign Henry. Coldstream Guards
Joined Coldstream Guards 1812. Helped to close the gates at Hougoumont. Promoted to Captain 1819. Retired as Lt-Colonel 1841.

GRAHAM, Corporal James. Coldstream Guards
Came from County Monaghan. A particularly strong man, he distinguished himself at the closing of the gates at Hougoumont. Then rescued his brother from a burning building. Was nominated for the annuity offered by the Rector of Framlingham for 'the most deserving soldier at Waterloo'. Was also given half the £500 awarded to Lt Colonel Macdonell as 'the bravest man in England' and a special medal for his gallantry. Retired 1816. Died 1843.

HEPBURN, Colonel Francis. Third Guards
Joined Third Guards 1794. Served in Peninsular War. Wounded at Barrosa 1811, and was awarded Gold Medal at Vitoria 1813. Commanded 2nd Battalion Third Guards at Waterloo, and took over 2nd Guards Brigade during the battle. Inadvertently failed to receive any mention in Wellington's Despatch. Rose to Major General. C.B. Retired 1821. Died 1835.

HOME, Lt-Colonel Francis. Third Guards
Joined Third Guards 1803. Served in Peninsular War. Commanded

Grenadier Company at Waterloo. Fought alongside Lt-Colonel Macdonell inside Hougoumont. Retired 1818.

MACDONELL, Lt-Colonel James. Coldstream Guards
Third son of Duncan Macdonell of Glengarry. Joined 19th Foot 1796.
Joined Coldstream Guards as Captain 1811. Awarded Gold Medal for
Maida 1806. Served in Peninsular War. Commanded Light Company
of 2nd Battalion Coldstream Guards at Waterloo. Was in command of
all troops inside Hougoumont, and distinguished himself at the closing
of the gates. Was slightly wounded. Awarded C.B. and K.M.T.[2] for
services at Waterloo. Rose to Major-General. Retired 1830. G.C.B.
and K.C.H.[2] Colonel-in-Chief of 71st (Highland Light Infantry.) Died
1859.

McGREGOR, Sergeant Bruce. Third Guards
Joined Third Guards in 1799. Served in 2nd Battalion at Waterloo.
Helped with the closing of the gates at Hougoumont. Retired 1822.
Became a Yeoman of the Guard. Died 1846.

MAITLAND, Major-General Peregrine. First Guards
Joined the First Guards in 1792. Commanded 1st Guards Brigade at
the Battle of the Nive 1813, at Quatre Bras and Waterloo. Distinguished
himself at the repulse the French Imperial Guard. Made a K.C.B.
22nd June 1815. Also received Russian Order of St Vladimir and Dutch
Order of Wilhelm. C-in-C at Madras 1836. Governor and C-in-C at
Cape of Good Hope 1843. Colonel-in-Chief 17th Foot 1843. Died
1854.

SALTOUN, Lt-Colonel Lord Alexander. First Guards
Son of Alexander Fraser, 15th Lord Saltoun. Joined First Guards 1804
from 42nd Foot. Commanded both Light Companies of 1st Guards
Brigade at Waterloo in the orchard at Hougoumont, and greatly dis-
tinguished himself. Had four horses shot under him, and two thirds of
his men were casualties. Was also prominent in the repulse of the
Imperial Guard.
   K.T. K.C.B. G.C.H. K.M.T. K.St G. Rose to Lieutenant General.
Colonel-in-Chief 2nd Foot 1846–53. Died 1853.

SEYMOUR, Lt-Colonel Horace. 18th Hussars
On the Staff at Waterloo and an ADC to Lord Uxbridge. Known as

[2] K.M.T. Knight of Maria Theresa of Austria.
   K.C.H. Knight Commander of Hanover.

'the strongest man in the British Army'. Transferred to First Life Guards in 1815. Retired 1819. Died 1851.

WOODFORD, Lt-Colonel Alexander. Coldstream Guards
Joined Coldstream Guards 1799. Served in the Peninsular War, where he won a Gold Medal and clasp. Commanded 2nd Battalion Coldstream Guards at Waterloo. Had a younger brother, Lt Colonel John Woodford, on the staff at Waterloo. Was in Hougoumont most of the afternoon, but declined to take over from Macdonell, although senior to him. Awarded C.B. for Waterloo. Became a Field Marshal. K.M.T. K.St G. Colonel-in-Chief 40th Foot 1842. Became Colonel Scots Fusilier Guards (formerly Third Guards) in 1861. Died 1870.

WYNDHAM, Lt-Colonel Henry. Coldstream Guards
Natural son of 3rd Earl of Egremont. Joined Coldstream Guards 1814 as Captain. Served in the Peninsular War. Commanded Light Company at Waterloo. Helped to close the gates at Hougoumont. Rose to General. Became Colonel-in-Chief 11th Hussars. K.C.B. MP for Cumberland. Succeeded to Egremont estates 1845. Died 1860.

Allied troops involved in the defence of Hougoumont

Division	Brigade	Units Involved	Strength
1st British (Major General George Cooke)	1st Guards (Major General Peregrine Maitland)	2nd Bn First Guards (light company only)	75
		3rd Bn First Guards (light company only)	90
	2nd Guards (Major General Sir John Byng)	2nd Bn Coldstream Guards	1,045
		2nd Bn Third Guards	1,056
2nd Netherlands (Lt General Baron de Perponcher)	2nd Nassau (Prince Bernard of Saxe-Weimar)	1st Bn, 2nd Nassau Regiment	600
3rd British (Lt General Sir Charles Alten)	1st Hanoverian (Major General Count von Kielmansegge)	1st Luneberg Bn (One company only)	100
		One Company from the Jäger Corps	321
2nd British (Lt General Sir Henry Clinton)	1st King's German Legion (Colonel G. du Plat)	1st K.G.L. Line Bn	411
		2nd ” ”	437
		3rd ” ”	494
		4th ” ”	416
	3rd Hanoverian (Colonel Hew Halkett)	Bremenvorde Landwehr Bn	632
		Osnabruck ” ”	612
		Quackenbruck ” ”	588
		Salzgitte ” ”	622
			7,499

Allied Artillery Involved in the Defence of Hougoumont

Unit	6 Pounders	9 Pounders	$5\frac{1}{2}$ inch Howitzers	Total Guns
Royal Horse Artillery				
Captain Ramsay's Troop	–	5	1	6
Major Bull's Troop	–	–	6	6
Lt Colonel Webber-Smith's Troop	5	–	1	6
Royal Field Artillery				
Captain's Bolton's Battery	–	5	1	6
Captain Sandham's ,,	–	5	1	6
King's German Legion Artillery				
Major Sympher's Troop	–	5	1	6
Captain Cleeve's Battery	–	5	1	6
Total Guns	**5**	**25**	**12**	**42**

French Forces Engaged Against Hougoumont

II Corps d'Armée. Lt General Count Reille

Division	Brigade	Commander	Regiments	Strength
5th Division				4,060
(Lt General Bachelu)	1st	Husson	2nd Light 61st Line	
	2nd	Campi	72nd Line 108th Line	
6th Division				5,680
(Lt General Prince Jerome)	1st	Bauduin	1st Light 3rd Line	
	2nd	Soye	1st Line 2nd Line	

Division	Brigade	Commander	Regiments	Strength
7th Division (Lt General Girard)		Left at Ligny		
9th Division				4,160
(Lt General Foy)	1st	Gauthier	92nd Line 93rd Line	
	2nd	Jamin	4th Light 100th Line	
2nd Cavalry Division				1,380
(Lt General Piré)	1st	Hubert	1st Chasseurs 6th Chasseurs	
	2nd	Wathiez	5th Lancers 6th Lancers	
Artillery			30 Guns	
Total Strength				13,900
				15,280

Selected Bibliography

BERNARD. Henri	Le Duc de Wellington et la Belgique	La Renaissance du Livre. 1983
BRETT-JAMES. Anthony	The Hundred Days	Sidgwick and Jackson. 1964
CHALFONT. Lord	Waterloo. The Battle of Three Armies	Sidgwick and Jackson. 1979
COTTON. Edward	A Voice from Waterloo	Various. 1847–1913
FLEISCHMANN, Hector	La Tragique Histoire du Chateau D'Hougoumont	Publié pour 'Les Amis de Waterloo.' 1913
GURWOOD. Lt Colonel	The Despatches of Field Marshal the Duke of Wellington. Vol XII	London. 1845
HAMILTON. Sir F. W.	The Origin and History of the First or Grenadier Guards	London. 1874
HOUSSAYE. Henri	1815. Waterloo	Translated by A. E. Mann. London 1987
LOGIE. Jacques	Waterloo. L'Évitable Défaite	Duclot. 1984
LONGFORD. Elizabeth	The Years of the Sword	Weidenfeld & Nicolson. 1969.
MACKINNON. Daniel	History of the Coldstream Guards	London. 1835
NAYLOR. John	Waterloo	Batsford. 1960
SAUNDERS. D. P.	Excavations at Hougoumont. 1978–1985	Journal of the Friends of the Waterloo Committee
SAUNDERS. Edith	The Hundred Days	Longmans, Green and Co. 1964
SIBORNE. H. T.	The Waterloo Letters	Arms and Armour Press. 1983
SIBORNE. William	The Waterloo Campaign	Constable and Co. 1895

| WELLER. Jac Association du Musée de Braine-l'Alleud | Wellington at Waterloo Braine-l'Alleud et son Histoire | London. 1967 Braine-l'Alleud. 1982 |

Index

Entries in bold refer to Hougoumont.

Cavalry – *contd.*
    French, 12, 17, 20, 28, 34, 36, 40,
        59–60, 62, 87, 91, 94, 102
Chapel, 8–9, 53–4, 72, 74–5, 78–81,
    82–3
Charleroi, 15, 16, 23
Chateau, 3, 7–9, 25, 27–8, 44–6, 53–
    4, 70–2, 74–5, 78, 80–1, 82–3
Clay, Private M., 27, 42, 56, 66, 70,
    80, 87, 90, 96
Cleeve, Captain, 36, 51, 101
Clinton, Lieutenant-General Sir H.,
    100
Colborne, Colonel J., 52n, 64
Coldstream Guards, 2, 26–30, 33, 36,
    37, 41–6, 47–9, 51n, 52, 53, 57–
    8, 58n, 60, 62, 67–9, 71, 73, 78,
    83, 85, 86, 88, 90, 91–5, 97, 98,
    99, 100, 103
Colville, Lieutenant-General Sir J.,
    23–4
Commissariat, 30, 34
Cooke, Major-General G., 23–4, 25,
    51, 91, 96, 100
Cotton, Sergeant-Major E., 85–6,
    103
Courtyard, 7, 8, 9, 78
Craufurd, Captain T., 78, 85
Cubières, Colonel, 41–2, 89, 97

Dashwood, Lieutenant-Colonel C.,
    28, 41, 96
D'Erlon, Lieutenant-General D., 20,
    21, 49, 50, 93
Despatches, 37, 52, 68, 97, 103
Divisions, Allied,
    1st British, 20, 22–4, 25, 36n, 51–2,
        96, 100
    2nd British, 20, 22, 100
    2nd Netherland, 100
    3rd British, 20, 22, 23, 48, 100
    4th British, 23–4
    5th British, 20, 23
    6th British, 20
Door, West, 9–11, 47, 78, 90
Double Rank, 28n, 72–3
D'Oultremont, Comtesse, 73
Drummond, Ensign B., 57–8, 97
Du Plat, Colonel G., 62

Evelyn, Captain G., 29, 91–2, 97

Farm, 7, 9, 25, 27–8, 33, 41–6, 53,
    62, 70–2, 74, 77, 78, 81–95
Farmyard, 7, 9, 25, 27–8, 33, 41–6,
    78, 79–81
First Guards (Grenadier Guards), 2,
    26–30, 31–3, 37, 39–40, 41, 49–
    50, 59, 63–4, 67, 78, 83, 86–7, 91–
    5, 96, 98, 100, 103
Fleischmann, H., 86, 103
Forbes, Captain H., 29–30
Foy, Lieutenant-General, 11, 20, 48,
    60, 61, 62, 68, 94, 95, 102
Fraser, Sergeant R., 41–2, 45–6, 73,
    79–80, 89, 97
French Troops, 15, 16, 34, 65, 85–6,
    101–2

Gann, Private, 42–3, 90
Garden, Formal, 3, 9–12, 28, 33, 41,
    48, 54, 57, 60, 78, 83–6, 89, 92
Garden, Small, 9–11, 78
Gardener, 25, 57, 70, 72
Gate, Garden, 9–11, 45, 78, 83
Gate, Great, See 'North Gate.'
Gate, North, 3, 9–11, 29, 41–6, 47,
    57, 77–81, 90
Gate, South, 9–11, 38, 39, 71, 74, 78,
    87, 88–90
Gates, Closing of the, 3, 10, 40, 41–6,
    53, 73, 90, 92, 97, 98, 99
Gautier, Brigadier-General, 11, 48,
    93, 102
Genappe, 16, 20
Girard, Lieutenant-General, 102
Gooch, Ensign H., 45–6, 56–7
Graham, Corporal James, 46, 53–4,
    73, 97
Graham, Corporal Joseph, 45–6, 53–4
Grenadier Companies, 27, 97
Grenadier Guards, See 'First
    Guards.'
Grouchy, Marshal, 16, 19, 40n
Guard, Imperial, 1, 20, 52n, 61, 62–
    3, 63n, 64, 65, 87, 95, 98
Guards, The, 1–2, 27n, 57, 63–9, 72–
    3, 83